VEGAN ROASTING PAN

VEGAN ROASTING PAN

Katy Beskow

LET YOUR OVEN DO THE HARD WORK
FOR YOU, WITH 70 SIMPLE ONE-PAN RECIPES

Photography by Luke Albert

Hardie Grant

QUADRILLE

Introduction

When it comes to preparing dinner, I aim to spend as little time as possible in the kitchen. Just like you, I have better things to be getting on with after a busy day of work or play. That doesn't mean sacrificing on flavour, nutrition or substance, but simply finding a way to cook with as little effort as possible. Having a mountain of pots and pans to wash up is also big no-no!

Enter *Vegan Roasting Pan*, 70 recipes that are cooked in just one dish. Say goodbye to pans boiling over on the stove, because cooking is about to get a whole lot easier: with a roasting pan and a few select pieces of preparation equipment.

Instead of standing over the stove, stirring, frying or flipping, simply pop your ingredients into a roasting pan, set a timer, then relax for a while. Not only is oven cooking in just one dish incredibly easy, but it gives food all those wonderful roasted and toasted flavours that methods like boiling just can't deliver.

It is often thought that vegan cooking is complicated, from sourcing ingredients to preparing them and turning them into something delicious; however, I firmly believe that vegan cooking is easy, fast and simple. Vegan foods are now widely available in supermarkets, with quality alternatives to familiar items that can be added to your favourite meals. As much as I advocate cooking from scratch, there is no harm in using some ready-prepared ingredients to make the cooking process as effortless as possible.

In this book, the recipes are organized into four chapters:

Light – Dishes that are simple enough for lunch, or a light supper.

Supper – Delicious and hearty one-pots that all of the family will love, any night of the week.

Extras – Sides and snacks that are easy to prepare.

Sweet – Bakes, puddings and breakfast ideas that are both simple and tasty.

To make the process even easier, I've included a tip with each recipe, and noted whether the dish is suitable for freezing, so you can prepare your meals in advance if batch cooking, or freeze any leftovers afterwards to reduce food waste.

My aim with all of the cookbooks I write is to reduce the amount of time you need to spend in the kitchen, simplify cooking processes, and prove that vegan cooking is easy. I hope this book helps to build your confidence in the kitchen, with fail-safe meals that all of the family will love, time and time again.

Whether you are a kitchen pro, or a vegan beginner, it's time to let your oven do all of the hard work! I hope you enjoy these recipes as much I have enjoyed creating them.

From my kitchen to yours, love Katy.

Which roasting pan?

Whether you choose aluminium, stainless steel, stoneware, cast-iron or glass, any of these materials are capable of transmitting heat through the ingredients effectively. The key to cooking in a roasting pan is to spread the ingredients out so they are able to roast, rather than steam, which will require a large roasting pan, or alternatively, two smaller.

Deep roasting pans circulate heat effectively, and are particularly useful when adding any liquid (such as wine, coconut milk or passata) to contain the ingredients without spillage. Consider large lasagne dishes or ovenproof casserole dishes if you don't specifically have a deep roasting pan.

Baking trays or sheets are almost flat, and are perfect for most types of baking, or cooking small amounts of food that don't require liquid retention. Spread out the topping for cherry and almond crumble (page 144) on a baking sheet for even colour and crispness.

Muffin trays (pans) are not just for baking muffins! Use them to make mini asparagus frittatas (page 45) or fajita bites (page 44) to create perfectly shaped, even portions. Opt for deep muffin trays, which usually have six holes, rather than the shallower bun trays.

Extra equipment

Kitchen foil is needed for some recipes in this book, to help the ingredients to cook by steaming and keep them moist and tender without drying out. It is also useful to ensure a more even cooking environment in a roasting pan, which will prevent some ingredients becoming overcooked while others are still cooking, particularly when the foil is wrapped loosely around the roasting pan.

Baking parchment helps to prevent ingredients sticking to the base of the roasting pan, and is designed to withstand high oven temperatures. Silicone sheets are useful to prevent cooked food sticking to the base of the roasting pan too; however, they can interfere with the transmission of heat, leaving some pieces of food undercooked.

Mixing bowls are useful for whisking together wet or dry ingredients, and to ensure vegetables, pulses and other ingredients are evenly coated in oil, juices and seasonings before going into the roasting pan.

A measuring jug is important when adding liquids to the roasting pan, and other ingredients can be added to it at that stage, to save on extra washing-up!

A high-powered blender or a food processor is useful for blitzing up dry coatings or sauces for your one-pan meal, with minimal effort required by you. You can also use it to blend roasted leftovers with vegetable stock to make a hearty soup the following day!

LOVE YOUR OVEN

1 Every oven is different, so it's worth getting to know whether your oven is slightly hotter or cooler than average. This comes with observation, and of course using the temperature setting accurately. All of the recipes in this book have been tested using a fan oven; if you are cooking with a conventional oven, a good rule of thumb is to increase the temperature stated in this book by 20 degrees celsius.

2 Don't overcrowd your oven with too many dishes and pans at once – for maximum effectiveness, clear other roasting pans or equipment that you might store in your oven. This way the heat can circulate efficiently, using less energy and less time, and will cook the food thoroughly.

3 Keep the oven door closed throughout (unless stated in the recipe, which is usually for turning food or adding other ingredients) as peeking in through the open door will dramatically reduce the temperature, which means your food will take longer to cook, and the quality may be affected – this is especially true with cakes.

4 Always preheat the oven to the temperature suggested, so when you place the roasting pan in the oven, the food will start cooking immediately without risking uneven heating or increased cooking times. Depending on your oven, this could take between 5–15 minutes.

5 Keep your oven clean, including the oven door, so you can see how your bake is cooking without having to open the door. As a rule, wipe the door with a cloth while the oven is just warm after cooking, or if your oven needs a deep clean, use one of the many vegan degreasing formulas or pastes available.

Useful ingredients

FRESH VEGETABLES AND FRUITS

Choose good-quality vegetables and fruit, particularly ones that attract you with a vibrant colour and fragrance. Eating seasonally will ensure you don't get stuck in a rut with the same produce, as it offers variety, new flavours and inspiration for a range of different recipes. Not only are vegetables and fruit good for the body, but they are easy to prepare and cook, versatile in their uses, and gentle on the pocket, especially when eaten in season.

When using citrus fruits, including lemons, limes and oranges, buy unwaxed varieties. Citrus fruits are often coated with a wax for aesthetic purposes to give them additional shine. This wax can often contain shellac, or other animal ingredients, making it unsuitable for vegans.

As the vegetables or fruits mentioned in these recipes will be baked in the oven, some of them can be substituted with their frozen counterparts. I have listed where this is possible, without compromising on flavour or quality.

OIL

I like to cook with sunflower oil, as it has a neutral flavour, high smoke point and is readily available for a good price. It can be substituted with vegetable oil or all-purpose olive oil if that is what you have available. Save extra virgin olive oil for drizzling and dressing finished dishes, to make the most of its green and fruity flavour.

PULSES, BEANS AND GRAINS

To reduce extra cooking steps, time and effort, I've used canned pulses and beans throughout (except for red split lentils as they require no pre-cooking or preparation). Canned pulses and beans are easy to store in the cupboard as they have a long shelf life, often have no added preservatives other than salt, and are easy to use when time is of the essence. Ensure you drain and rinse the beans or pulses thoroughly, to remove any 'canned' flavour. Vacuum-packed grains such as quinoa can be easily sourced in supermarkets, and remove the need to soak and boil before enjoying.

NUTS

Nuts become toasted and flavoursome when cooked in the oven, as well as adding crunch and texture. I love using peanuts, cashews and pistachios for maximum flavour, minimal effort and added protein.

PASTA

Many brands of dried pasta available in supermarkets are egg-free, but always check the ingredients before you buy. Fresh pasta (or that which you'll find in the chilled aisle) is likely to contain eggs, making it unsuitable for vegans. Pasta is a great store cupboard essential, not just for use in pasta bakes, but in hearty soups and stews.

RICE

Basmati rice releases a distinctive fragrance during cooking and has the benefit of a speedy cooking time and even shape, meaning it cooks evenly and well when steamed in the oven with the appropriate amount of liquid.

HERBS, SPICES AND SPICE BLENDS

Alongside your favourite basic dried herbs and spices, choose a few pre-blended mixes that will save you shelf space instead of having to stock lots of individual ingredients. These may include dried mixed herbs, curry paste and rose harissa paste. As a rule, woody herbs such as sage, rosemary and thyme taste great when dried, but buy fresh leafy herbs such as flat-leaf parsley, basil and coriander for the best flavour.

VEGAN CHEESE, BUTTER, MILK AND YOGURT

Non-dairy cheeses, butter, milk and yogurts are now readily available in supermarkets. Soya and oat milk are particularly versatile for use in cooking, with a neutral flavour and creamy mouthfeel. Vegan cream cheese is an excellent ingredient for cooking, spreading and baking, with many varieties to try. Plain soya yogurt or thick coconut yogurt can be used in both savoury or sweet dishes. Where coconut milk is used in this book, it refers to the full-fat canned variety.

SUGAR

I take a common-sense approach to using sugar; you'll find it in some of the sweet recipes, and a small amount to reduce the acidity of tomato-based dishes. Enjoy in moderation!

SEA SALT AND BLACK PEPPER

For the best pops of flavour, sprinkle good-quality sea salt flakes over food after cooking. Used in moderation, sea salt will lift any dish and enhance the roasted flavours. Add freshly ground black pepper to taste as preferred.

Soy-roasted broccoli, sugarsnap peas & green beans

with sesame, lime & chilli

SERVES 2 GENEROUSLY

225g (8oz) Tenderstem broccoli

handful of sugarsnap peas, tough ends trimmed

handful of green beans, trimmed and roughly chopped

1 tsp sunflower oil

2 tbsp light soy sauce

pinch of dried chilli flakes

1 tbsp sesame seeds

zest of ½ unwaxed lime, finely grated

Broccoli takes on a hearty, smoky flavour when roasted, and is extra delicious when roasted with soy sauce, chilli and sesame seeds. Serve as a warm salad with fresh green leaves and coriander, or with fluffy coconut rice (page 121) for bigger appetites.

Preheat the oven to 200°C/400°F/gas mark 6.

Combine the broccoli, sugarsnap peas and green beans in a large bowl. Stir through the sunflower oil, soy sauce and chilli flakes until combined.

Lay the coated vegetables into a roasting pan and scatter with the sesame seeds. Roast in the oven for 12–15 minutes until the vegetables have softened and the seeds appear toasted.

Remove from the oven and stir through the lime zest. Serve warm.

EASY TIP:

This dish is a good alternative to a stir-fry when eaten for supper. Simply throw over some roasted cashews for extra substance.

Warm peach & basil salad

SERVES 2 GENEROUSLY

2 peaches, stoned and sliced

1 tsp sunflower oil

2 tbsp walnut halves

60g (2oz) wild rocket (arugula)

1 celery stick, finely chopped

2 tsp good-quality balsamic vinegar

handful of small basil leaves

Sweet roasted peaches, zesty basil, peppery rocket, crisp celery and toasted walnuts come together in this sweet and tangy salad. Especially good to revive those peaches left neglected in the fruit bowl.

Preheat the oven to 180°C/350°F/gas mark 4.

Lay the peach slices in a roasting pan and brush with a little sunflower oil. Roast in the oven for 10 minutes, then carefully scatter in the walnuts and cook for a further 5 minutes.

Meanwhile, combine the rocket, celery and balsamic vinegar in a bowl, then transfer to plates or a serving bowl.

Remove the roasted peaches and walnuts from the oven and lay over the dressed rocket. Scatter with basil leaves and serve warm.

EASY TIP:

Switch the peaches for seasonal soft fruits including plums, strawberries and blood oranges for new variations all year round.

Herby lentils & chickpeas

with lemon yogurt

SERVES 2

• SUITABLE FOR FREEZING
  (WITHOUT THE YOGURT)

1 x 400g (14oz) can green lentils, drained and rinsed

1 x 400g (14oz) can chickpeas (garbanzo beans), drained and rinsed

2 tbsp sunflower oil

1 tsp dried sage

handful of shelled pistachios, roughly chopped

seeds of 1 pomegranate

small handful of flat-leaf parsley, finely chopped

generous pinch of sea salt and black pepper

For the lemon yogurt

4 heaped tbsp plain soya yogurt, chilled

juice of ¼ unwaxed lemon

pinch of sea salt

This warm and herby dish is full of substance, flavour and fragrance. Serve warm in toasted pittas for a relaxed lunch, or chilled with salad leaves for the perfect packed lunch or picnic.

Preheat the oven to 180°C/350°F/gas mark 4.

In a bowl, stir together the lentils, chickpeas, oil, sage and pistachios. Pour into a deep roasting pan and cover loosely with foil.

Bake in the oven for 15–20 minutes until the lentils and chickpeas are hot and fragrant. Stir through the pomegranate seeds and flat-leaf parsley, then season to taste with salt and pepper.

To prepare the lemon yogurt, combine the yogurt, lemon and sea salt in a small bowl, then spoon over the herby lentils and chickpeas just before serving.

EASY TIP:

If you don't want the messy task of removing the juicy seeds from a pomegranate, many supermarkets sell prepared pomegranate seeds, saving you time and cleaning up!

Roasted cauliflower tacos

SERVES 4

2 tsp smoked paprika

1 tsp mild chilli powder

½ tsp ground cumin

pinch of dried oregano

pinch of dried chilli flakes

3 tbsp sunflower oil

1 large cauliflower, leaves removed, broken into bite-sized florets

1 red (bell) pepper, very thinly sliced

1 avocado, peeled, stoned and thinly sliced

small handful of coriander (cilantro) leaves, torn

generous pinch of sea salt

8 soft tortilla wraps or hard taco shells

unwaxed lime wedges, to serve

For Taco Tuesday and beyond! These roasted cauliflower and red pepper tacos are gently spiced and served with cooling avocado, coriander and lime. If I have them to hand, I like to serve this with pickled pink onions (see right) and vegan sour cream.

Preheat the oven to 180°C/350°F/gas mark 4.

In a bowl, stir together the smoked paprika, chilli powder, cumin, oregano and chilli flakes. Spoon in the sunflower oil and mix into a paste.

Put the cauliflower florets into a deep roasting pan and use a pastry brush to brush the spice paste liberally over the cauliflower. Add the red pepper slices and roast for 20–22 minutes until the pepper is softened and the florets are golden and gently roasted.

Remove the roasting pan from the oven and lay over the avocado slices. Scatter with coriander leaves and season with salt.

Load into taco shells or onto soft totillas and serve with a wedge of lime for squeezing.

EASY TIP:

You can make tortilla wraps into taco shells, if you like – simply brush with a little sunflower oil and hang over the bars of your oven shelf, baking for a few moments until crisp and ready for loading.

Quick-pickled onions

2 red onions, halved and thinly sliced

200ml (7fl oz) cider vinegar

1 tbsp maple syrup

½ tsp dried chilli flakes

zest of 1 unwaxed lime

generous pinch of sea salt

Make a batch of these and keep a jar in fridge to add a little zing to all sorts of one-pan meals.

Put the onion slices into a large bowl and pour over enough boiling water to cover completely. Leave to stand for 10 minutes. In a jug (pitcher), whisk together the vinegar and maple syrup, then stir in the chilli flakes, lime zest and sea salt. Drain the water from the onions and pat dry with kitchen paper. Pour over the vinegar mixture, then refrigerate for 1 hour before serving.

Sweet potato hash

SERVES 4

• SUITABLE FOR FREEZING

4 sweet potatoes, peeled and cut into 2cm (¾in) dice

1 red (bell) pepper, thinly sliced

1 red onion, finely chopped

drizzle of sunflower oil

½ tsp smoked paprika

pinch of dried chilli flakes

pinch of dried oregano

1 x 400g (14oz) can red kidney beans, drained and rinsed

generous pinch of smoked sea salt

handful of fresh chives, finely chopped

1 avocado, peeled, stoned and thinly sliced

Enjoy this hearty hash for breakfast, brunch and beyond! Feel free to leave out the chilli flakes for younger diners, or throw over some sliced green chilli or Tabasco if you like it hot.

Preheat the oven to 200°C/400°F/gas mark 6.

Arrange the sweet potatoes, pepper and red onion in a deep roasting pan and drizzle with sunflower oil. Sprinkle over the smoked paprika, chilli flakes and oregano and stir through.

Roast in the oven for 30 minutes, then carefully remove the roasting pan from the oven. Tip in the red kidney beans and stir through to distribute evenly. Carefully return the pan to the oven for a further 8–10 minutes.

Remove from the oven and season with smoked sea salt. Scatter with chopped chives and lay over the slices of avocado just before serving.

EASY TIP:

Blend any leftovers with some vegetable stock and a squeeze of lime juice, for a Mexican-style soup the next day.

Sticky maple aubergine

with crushed peanuts

SERVES 2

2 tbsp sunflower oil

2 tbsp maple syrup

1 tbsp light soy sauce

2 garlic cloves, crushed

1 large aubergine (eggplant), sliced lenthways into about 4 strips

1 tsp sesame seeds

1 spring onion (scallion), finely sliced into slivers

small handful of coriander (cilantro) leaves, roughly torn

2 tbsp salted peanuts, roughly chopped

Sweet and savoury flavours of maple and soy sauce give an eastern twist to roasted aubergine. Serve with noodles, simple stir-fried greens or a crisp carrot salad for a satisfying lunch or light dinner.

Preheat the oven to 180°C/350°F/gas mark 4.

In a bowl, whisk together the oil, maple syrup, soy sauce and crushed garlic until combined.

Use a knife to make criss-cross incisions into each aubergine slice, making sure you don't cut all the way through.

Add the strips of aubergine and toss to coat in the maple-soy marinade. Arrange the coated strips in a roasting pan and roast for 30–35 minutes until the aubergine has softened and become sticky.

Remove from the oven and scatter with the sesame seeds, spring onion, coriander and peanuts.

Pictured overleaf

EASY TIP:

For an extra kick, scatter over some chopped red chilli and a squeeze of lime juice before serving.

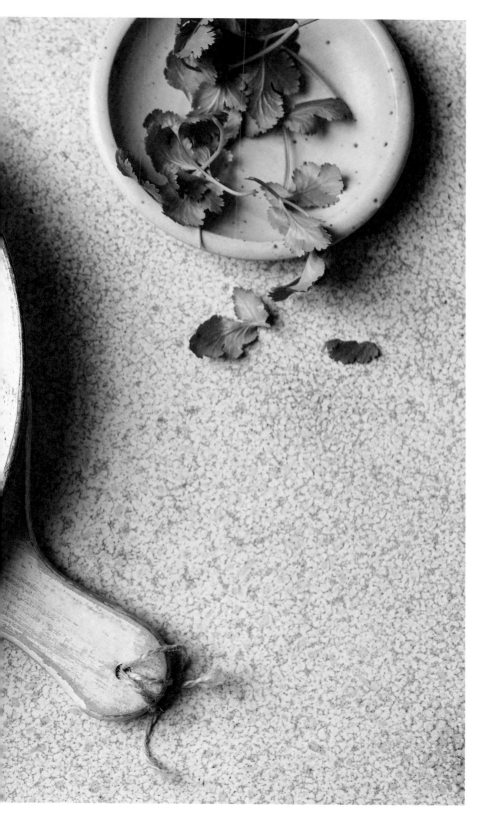

Sticky maple
aubergine
with crushed
peanuts

Hot ALT sandwiches

SERVES 2

1 tbsp barbecue sauce (ensure vegan)

1 aubergine (eggplant), thinly sliced into rasher strips

pinch of dried oregano

6 cherry tomatoes

1 small red onion, thinly sliced

drizzle of sunflower oil

4 thick slices of sourdough bread

1 tsp vegan butter

2 tsp vegan mayonnaise

½ baby gem lettuce, leaves separated, tough stem discarded

pinch of smoked sea salt

Smoky aubergine rashers, lettuce, roasted tomato, red onion and fresh sourdough – and all in one roasting pan. Lunch is served!

Preheat the oven to 180°C/350°F/gas mark 4.

Brush a little barbecue sauce over each strip of aubergine and place in a single layer in a deep roasting pan. Scatter with a pinch of oregano.

Add the cherry tomatoes and red onion slices to the roasting pan. Drizzle with sunflower oil then roast in the oven for 25–30 minutes until the aubergine is slightly crisp at the edges and the onion slices have softened.

Lay out the slices of bread and butter them right to the edges. Spread 2 of the slices with a little vegan mayonnaise then top with the lettuce leaves.

Remove the roasting pan from the oven and season with smoked sea salt. Spoon the aubergine rashers, roasted tomatoes and onions on top of the lettuce and sandwich with the other slices of bread.

EASY TIP:

Use a sharp knife to slice the aubergine into thin slices – the thinner the slice, the crispier the smoked aubergine 'rashers' will be!

Greek-style baked beans

SERVES 2 GENEROUSLY

• SUITABLE FOR FREEZING

500g (2 cups) passata

2 tbsp tomato purée (paste)

pinch of sugar

1 tsp dried oregano

1 garlic clove, crushed

1 x 400g (14oz) can butterbeans, drained and rinsed

handful of pitted black olives

1 bay leaf

handful of flat-leaf parsley, finely chopped

small handful of fresh dill, finely chopped

generous pinch of sea salt and black pepper

juice of ¼ unwaxed lemon, to serve

Butterbeans, olives, sweet tomato sauce and fresh herbs combine in this Greek-style one-pot. Serve with toasted sourdough or over a baked potato, with a spoonful of vegan plain yogurt, if you like.

Preheat the oven to 180°C/350°F/gas mark 4.

In a bowl, whisk together the passata, tomato purée, sugar, oregano and garlic. Stir in the butterbeans and olives until coated in the mixture.

Pour the butterbean mix into a deep roasting pan and lay in the bay leaf. Cover loosely with foil, then bake in the oven for 35–40 minutes.

Remove from the oven and discard the bay leaf. Scatter in the parsley and dill, then season with salt and pepper. Squeeze over the lemon juice just before serving.

EASY TIP:

Butterbeans are my favourite to use for this recipe, however cannellini, haricot or canned mixed beans are good alternatives.

Harissa flatbreads

with roasted tomatoes

SERVES 2

300g (10oz) cherry
tomatoes

1 small red onion,
very finely chopped

drizzle of sunflower oil

2 flatbreads (ensure
dairy-free)

2 rounded tsp harissa
paste

small handful of flat-leaf
parsley, finely chopped

generous pinch of sea
salt

Refresh shop-bought flatbreads with harissa, roasted tomatoes and red onions, and a scatter of flat-leaf parsley. A full-of-flavour lunch that is ready in under 30 minutes.

Preheat the oven to 200°C/400°F/gas mark 6.

Arrange the tomatoes and red onion in a roasting pan and drizzle with sunflower oil. Roast in the oven for 15 minutes.

Meanwhile, lay out the flatbreads on a clean surface and spread evenly with the harissa, 1 teaspoon per flatbread. Carefully place the flatbreads in the oven to heat for 5 minutes.

Remove the roasting pan and the flatbreads from the oven and spoon the roasted tomatoes and onions over the flatbreads. Scatter with chopped parsley and season with salt.

EASY TIP:

Use a pastry brush to spread the harissa onto the flatbreads, for easy and even distribution.

Watermelon niçoise

SERVES 2

½ watermelon, cut into 3cm (1¼in) chunks

½ tsp nori seasoning

2 baby gem lettuces, sliced into wedges

handful of black olives, pitted

6 cherry tomatoes, halved

handful of basil leaves

generous drizzle of good-quality extra virgin olive oil

pinch of sea salt and black pepper

wedges of unwaxed lemon, to serve

We all know that watermelon is delicious when sliced straight from the skin, but roasting and serving it warm intensifies the sweetness and melt-in-the-mouth texture. Sprinkle with nori seasoning or flakes for an added taste of the sea. Serve with wedges of crusty bread or new potatoes.

Preheat the oven to 180°C/350°F/gas mark 4.

Arrange the watermelon cubes in a roasting pan and scatter over the nori seasoning. Bake in the oven for 15–20 minutes until hot.

Meanwhile, arrange the lettuce wedges in a bowl and scatter over the olives, tomatoes and basil leaves. Drizzle with olive oil and season with salt and pepper.

Remove the watermelon from the oven and toss into the salad. Serve with wedges of lemon to squeeze over.

Pictured overleaf

EASY TIP:

Nori (seaweed) seasoning can be found in many supermarkets, often in the world food aisle.

Watermelon
niçoise

Marinated & roasted courgettes

with antipasti & toast

SERVES 2

1 tbsp sunflower oil

zest and juice of
1 unwaxed lemon

1 garlic clove, lightly
bashed

pinch of dried chilli
flakes

small handful of flat-leaf
parsley, very finely
chopped

2 large courgettes
(zucchini), very thinly
sliced into ribbons (see
Easy Tip on page 82)

small handful of mint
leaves, very finely
chopped

2 tsp pine nuts

handful of pitted black
olives

4 sundried tomatoes in
oil, drained and roughly
sliced

4 artichokes in oil,
drained and roughly
sliced

generous pinch of sea
salt and black pepper

thin slices of toasted
sourdough bread, to
serve

**Make courgettes the star of the show in this
fresh lunch. They can be marinated overnight
but if making the same day leave them for at
least an hour, to absorb the vibrant flavours of
lemon, chilli and parsley.**

In a bowl, whisk together the oil, lemon zest and
juice, garlic, chilli flakes and parsley. Stir in the
courgette ribbons and allow to marinate for at
least 1 hour.

Preheat the oven to 180°C/350°F/gas mark 4.

Arrange the courgettes evenly in a roasting pan,
then roast in the oven for 10 minutes.

Remove from the oven and scatter with the
chopped mint, pine nuts, olives, sundried
tomatoes and artichokes. Season with salt
and pepper and toss everything together.

Arrange on a serving platter, spooning over
any residual oil from the pan. Serve with
sourdough toast.

EASY TIP:

The courgettes are wonderful either hot or at
room temperature, and a perfect addition to
any al fresco lunch.

Roasted spring salad

SERVES 2

10 new potatoes, halved

2 carrots, peeled and cut into rounds

handful of radishes

drizzle of sunflower oil

8–10 asparagus spears, woody ends trimmed

250g (9oz) cooked quinoa

small handful of coriander (cilantro), chopped

juice of ½ unwaxed lemon

generous pinch of sea salt and black pepper

New potatoes, carrots, asparagus and radishes are the jewels of springtime, but when they spend some time roasting in the oven, the flavours intensify and become doubly delicious. A lovely lunch for a cooler spring day. Serve warm, or keep in the fridge for a tasty lunchbox salad the next day.

Preheat the oven to 200°C/400°F/gas mark 6.

Tip the potatoes, carrots and radishes into a deep roasting pan and spread out evenly, then drizzle with sunflower oil. Roast in the oven for 30 minutes, or until soft.

Carefully remove the roasting pan from the oven and throw in the asparagus. Roast for a further 8–10 minutes until the asparagus is tender.

Remove the roasting pan from the oven and stir in the quinoa and chopped coriander, then squeeze over the lemon juice. Toss and season to taste with salt and pepper.

EASY TIP:

Cooked quinoa can be found in handy pouches in most supermarkets, making it a convenient and nutritious addition to any lunch or supper.

BBQ cauliflower wings

with roasted peppers & lime

SERVES 4

200ml (generous ¾ cup) barbecue sauce (ensure vegan)

2 tbsp sunflower oil

½ tsp dried chilli flakes

100g (2 cups) panko breadcrumbs

1 medium cauliflower, broken into bite-sized florets with some stem remaining

1 red (bell) pepper, thinly sliced

1 unwaxed lime, halved

handful of fresh chives, finely chopped

2 tbsp vegan mayonnaise, chilled, to serve

These wings are crispy on the outside and juicy on the inside, with a spicy barbecue sauce – delicious with roasted peppers and a squeeze of lime. Serve with warmed tortilla wraps, if you like.

Preheat the oven to 200°C/400°F/gas mark 6.

In a large bowl, mix together the barbecue sauce, oil and chilli flakes until combined.

Arrange the panko breadcrumbs on a plate. Dip the cauliflower florets into the barbecue sauce mix, shake off any excess, then roll in the panko breadcrumbs. When the florets are coated, place in a roasting pan. Repeat until each floret is coated.

Add the pepper slices and halved lime to the pan and bake in the oven for 15 minutes. Carefully remove from the oven and use tongs to turn the florets, then return to the oven for a further 10–15 minutes until the cauliflower wings are evenly golden.

Remove from the oven and scatter with the chives. Serve with vegan mayonnaise and squeeze over the warm lime juice, when the lime halves are cool enough to handle.

EASY TIP:

Roasting the lime allows for less sharpness, and a slightly charred lime flavour.

Fajita bites

MAKES 8

2 tsp sunflower oil

3 large tortilla wraps

2 tbsp tomato purée (paste)

1 tsp smoked paprika

pinch of dried oregano

pinch of mild chilli powder

1 yellow (bell) pepper, diced

2 spring onions (scallions), finely chopped

pinch of sea salt

small handful of coriander (cilantro) leaves

1 avocado, peeled, stoned and finely sliced

Enjoy these fun fajita bites as a quick lunch, served hot or cold, or as the perfect snack. Serve with a spoonful of vegan mayonnaise and a squeeze of lime juice.

Preheat the oven to 180°C/350°F/gas mark 4. Use a pastry brush to grease 8 holes of a deep muffin tin (pan) with sunflower oil, then set aside.

Lay out the tortilla wraps on a flat surface. Use a large cookie cutter (or just cut around a cup with a sharp knife) to press out 16 circles, large enough to fill each muffin hole.

Press one single tortilla round into each muffin hole, then brush the surface with a little oil. Press on another tortilla round to make a double layer.

In a bowl, stir together the tomato purée, smoked paprika, oregano, chilli powder, diced pepper and spring onions, then spoon the mix evenly into the tortilla cups.

Bake in the oven for 10 minutes until the edges are golden and the filling is bubbling.

Carefully remove from the oven and allow to cool for a couple of minutes. Season with a little salt, then top with the coriander and avocado slices. Use a teaspoon to lift the fajita bites from each hole and onto a serving plate.

EASY TIP:
The tortilla cups can be made in advance and kept in an airtight container for 2–3 days before filling with the fajita mix and baking until the filling is hot.

Mini asparagus frittatas

MAKES 6

• SUITABLE FOR FREEZING

½ tsp sunflower oil

1 x 280g (9½oz) block of extra-firm tofu, drained of excess moisture (no need to press)

¼ tsp ground turmeric

1 tbsp soya milk

small handful of flat-leaf parsley, very finely chopped

6 asparagus spears, woody ends trimmed, sliced lengthways

generous pinch of sea salt and black pepper

These delicate frittatas make the perfect lunch when served with a salad of peppery leaves and freshly podded peas. Tofu replaces eggs in these vegan frittatas, which will last for up to 2 days in the fridge. Best served warm.

Preheat the oven to 200°C/400°F/gas mark 6. Brush 6 holes of a muffin tin (pan) with a little sunflower oil.

Break the tofu up into a high-powered blender jug or food processor and spoon in the turmeric and soya milk. Add 3 tablespoons water and blitz on high, then add another 3 tablespoons water and blitz again to form a thick paste (it should be thick enough to spoon rather than pour). Stir through the chopped parsley and season with salt and plenty of pepper.

Spoon 2 tablespoons of the mix into each muffin hole. Place 2 halved asparagus spears on top of each frittata, pressing them down into the mixture a little.

Bake in the oven for 15 minutes, then reduce the heat to 180°C/350°F/gas mark 4 and bake for a further 5–7 minutes until the frittatas appear set. Remove from the oven and allow to stand for a few minutes before using a teaspoon to gently remove them from each muffin hole.

EASY TIP:

The batter can be made up to a day in advance and kept in the fridge; simply add a little extra water if it is too thick. Perfect for when you need to lunch and go (without extra washing up!).

Maple roasted fig & pecan salad

SERVES 2

4 figs, halved lengthways

1 tbsp maple syrup

1 small red onion, thinly sliced into rounds

small drizzle of sunflower oil

small handful of pecans

2 generous handfuls of rocket (arugula)

handful of flat-leaf parsley, torn

4 radishes, thinly sliced

juice of ¼ unwaxed lemon

Sweet, juicy figs with lightly toasted pecans come together in this elegant salad. Team with peppery rocket and radishes for contrast.

Preheat the oven to 180°C/350°F/gas mark 4.

Arrange the fig halves in a roasting pan and brush all over with maple syrup. Add the onion rounds and drizzle everything with a little sunflower oil. Roast in the oven for 15 minutes.

After 15 minutes, carefully add the pecans to the roasting pan and bake for a further 5 minutes.

Toss together the rocket, parsley, radishes and lemon juice in a bowl. Remove the roasting pan from the oven and stir through the roasted figs, onion and pecans.

EASY TIP:

This salad makes a delicious lunch, or serve as a side dish with my chickpea and olive orzo bake (page 92).

Butterbean, fennel & tomato bake

with orange & thyme

SERVES 2

2 fennel bulbs, sliced into even wedges

zest and juice of 1 unwaxed orange

drizzle of sunflower oil

500g (1lb 2oz) mixed baby tomatoes

leaves from 1 sprig of fresh thyme

1 x 400g (14oz) can butterbeans, drained and rinsed

generous pinch of sea salt and black pepper

This simple and delicious bake can be eaten either hot or cold, with some crusty bread. Fresh thyme is better than dried in this vibrant recipe.

Preheat the oven to 180°C/350°F/gas mark 4.

Lay the fennel wedges into a roasting pan and squeeze over the orange juice (reserve the zest for later). Drizzle with a little sunflower oil and roast in the oven for 30 minutes.

Carefully remove from the oven and stir in the tomatoes, thyme and orange zest. Return to the oven for a further 10 minutes.

After 10 minutes, stir in the butterbeans and cook for a further 5 minutes until the butterbeans are hot.

Remove from the oven and season to taste with salt and pepper.

EASY TIP:

Citrus fruits can often be waxed with animal ingredients, including shellac, making the waxed varieties unsuitable for vegans. Shop for unwaxed fruits, which will be stated on the label or packaging.

Sicilian caponata

SERVES 2

• SUITABLE FOR FREEZING

1 large aubergine (eggplant), sliced into half-rounds

1 red onion, thickly sliced

2 large tomatoes, sliced into rounds

pinch of dried oregano

drizzle of sunflower oil

4 tbsp balsamic vinegar

handful of pitted green olives

generous pinch of sea salt and black pepper

small handful of basil leaves

Caponata is often made by frying aubergine with other vegetables and a splash of balsamic vinegar to give it a sweet-sour flavour. Instead of bringing out the frying pan, throw the ingredients into a roasting pan and let the oven do all of the hard work. Delicious eaten hot from the oven, or at room temperature as a refreshing salad.

Preheat the oven to 180°C/350°F/gas mark 4.

Arrange the aubergine and red onion slices in a deep roasting pan and lay over the sliced tomatoes.

Scatter with the dried oregano and drizzle over the sunflower oil. Evenly spoon over the balsamic vinegar, then bake in the oven for 30–35 minutes until the aubergine is soft and starting to become golden.

Remove from the oven and scatter with the olives. Season with salt and pepper and toss with the basil leaves just before serving.

EASY TIP:

I love to keep caponata simple, but feel free to throw in sultanas, pine nuts and toasted almonds for extra texture and flavour.

Squash au vin

SERVES 4

• SUITABLE FOR FREEZING

1 butternut squash, deseeded and sliced into thin semi rounds

6 shallots, peeled and halved

1 carrot, peeled and thinly sliced into rounds

1 celery stick, thinly sliced

6 baby potatoes, halved

4 tbsp pearl barley

½ tsp dried sage

200ml (generous ¾ cup) red wine (ensure vegan)

200ml (generous ¾ cup) hot vegetable stock

1 bay leaf

generous pinch of sea salt and black pepper

If there's a one-pan dish that represents autumn, it is this squash au vin. Tender butternut squash, sage, roasted potatoes and plump pearl barley cook up into this comforting supper. Serve with crusty bread for dipping into the herby red wine sauce.

Preheat the oven to 180°C/350°F/gas mark 4.

Arrange the squash, shallots, carrot, celery and potatoes in a deep roasting pan. Scatter over the pearl barley and dried sage.

Pour in the red wine and vegetable stock so the pearl barley is covered, and tuck in the bay leaf.

Loosely cover with foil, then bake in the oven for 20 minutes. After 20 minutes, carefully remove the foil and stir. Increase the oven temperature to 200°C/400°F/gas mark 6 and cook for a further 1 hour, uncovered.

Remove from the oven and season to taste with salt and pepper.

EASY TIP:

There's no need to peel the butternut squash, simply scrub clean, then dry thoroughly before slicing.

Cauliflower cheese pie

SERVES 4

200ml (generous ¾ cup) unsweetened soya milk

150g (5oz) vegan cream cheese

generous handful of fresh chives, finely chopped

generous pinch of sea salt and black pepper

1 cauliflower, broken into florets

pinch of grated nutmeg

6 sheets of filo pastry (ensure dairy-free)

Combining two of the best comfort foods – cauliflower cheese and pie – this supper is creamy, cheesy and oh-so satisfying. I like to cook this in a round casserole dish, but it also works well in a medium-sized roasting pan. Serve with steamed greens and peas, if you like.

Preheat the oven to 180°C/350°F/gas mark 4.

In a jug or bowl, whisk together the soya milk and cream cheese until combined, then stir in the chives and season with salt and pepper.

Put the cauliflower into an ovenproof casserole dish or medium roasting pan, then pour in the cheese mixture. Sprinkle over the nutmeg, then bake in the oven for 30 minutes.

Remove from the oven. Unroll the pastry sheets and gently scrunch them, placing them over the top of the baked cauliflower. When you have completely covered the top with scrunched filo, return the dish or pan to the oven for a further 15–20 minutes until golden and crisp.

EASY TIP:

Many brands of shop-bought pastry, including filo, are already vegan as they contain vegetable oil instead of butter, but always check the label before you buy.

Parsnip, chestnut & cranberry bake

SERVES 2 GENEROUSLY

• SUITABLE FOR FREEZING

4 parsnips, peeled and sliced into 4cm (1½in) pieces

2 sweet potatoes, peeled and sliced into 4cm (1½in) pieces

1 red onion, peeled and quartered

drizzle of sunflower oil

generous pinch of dried sage

180g (6oz) vacuum-packed cooked chestnuts

handful of cranberries (fresh or frozen)

zest of ¼ unwaxed orange, grated

generous pinch of sea salt and black pepper

This warming winter roast is comforting, balanced and so easy to make. Perfect for serving on Boxing Day, to use up those Christmas leftovers. Delicious alone, or served with gravy.

Preheat the oven to 190°C/375°F/gas mark 5.

Place the parsnips, sweet potatoes and red onion into a deep roasting pan, ensuring they do not overlap. Drizzle with sunflower oil and scatter over the sage. Roast in the oven for 20 minutes.

Carefully remove from the oven and turn over the parsnips and sweet potatoes using tongs. Add the chestnuts and cranberries, then scatter over the orange zest. Return to the oven and roast for a further 15 minutes until the vegetables are golden and crisp.

Remove from the oven and season to taste with salt and pepper.

EASY TIP:

Vacuum-packed cooked chestnuts can be found in most supermarkets and are versatile for adding to casseroles, bakes, stuffing and stir-fries. They save the time and energy of roasting and peeling chestnuts, and last for a long time in the store cupboard.

Roasted mushroom burgers

with chargrilled peppers & basil mayonnaise

SERVES 2

1 tbsp balsamic vinegar

1 tsp sunflower oil

2 large flat mushrooms, stalks carefully removed, leaving the mushroom intact

2 jarred chargrilled peppers in oil, drained and roughly sliced

2 tbsp vegan mayonnaise

handful of basil leaves, finely chopped

2 burger buns (ensure vegan), sliced in half

pinch of sea salt and black pepper

small handful of watercress

These roasted mushrooms are juicy, tender and packed with flavours of reduced balsamic vinegar and charred peppers. Perfect to cook in the oven, or throw on the barbecue. The basil mayonnaise can be made in advance and kept refrigerated for up to 2 days.

Preheat the oven to 200°C/400°F/gas mark 6.

Whisk together the balsamic vinegar and sunflower oil in a bowl, then liberally brush over the mushrooms, including the base and middle hollow.

Lay the mushrooms in a roasting pan. Stuff the sliced chargrilled peppers into the hollow of each mushroom, then roast in the oven for 20 minutes.

Meanwhile, stir together the mayonnaise and chopped basil and allow to infuse for 15 minutes.

Warm the burger buns in the oven for a minute, then remove, along with the mushroom burgers. Season the burgers with salt and pepper.

Generously spread the base of each bun with the basil mayo, add a mushroom and pepper burger to each, followed by a handful of watercress, then top with the other bun half.

EASY TIP:

Jarred chargrilled peppers can be found in most supermarkets, and are a great way to pack in flavour to any meal without having to spend time grilling peppers. Keep a jar in the fridge and throw into a salad, chilli or bolognaise.

Oven-ready biryani

SERVES 4

400g (2 cups) basmati rice, rinsed

2 carrots, peeled and thinly sliced into rounds

½ cauliflower, broken into florets

10 green beans, trimmed and halved

generous handful of cashews

1 x 400ml (14fl oz) can coconut milk

1 tbsp medium curry paste (ensure dairy-free)

1 tsp ground turmeric

½ tsp ground cumin

½ tsp dried chilli flakes

2 spring onions (scallions), finely chopped

generous handful of coriander (cilantro) leaves, roughly torn

generous pinch of sea salt

juice of ½ unwaxed lemon, plus lemon wedges to serve

Lightly spiced biryani is a family favourite, and it is so simple to make in a deep roasting pan. Feel free to add any vegetables that you have available, such as sweetcorn, sugarsnap peas and cherry tomatoes.

EASY TIP:

Basmati rice has a fragrant aroma and the fluffy texture needed for this dish. Other types of rice will require a longer cooking time.

Preheat the oven to 200°C/400°F/gas mark 6.

Scatter the rice into a deep roasting pan, along with the carrots, cauliflower florets, green beans and cashews.

Pour the coconut milk into a jug (pitcher), along with 200ml (generous ¾ cup) water. Whisk in the curry paste, turmeric, cumin and chilli flakes until combined.

Pour the spiced coconut milk mix over the rice and gently stir through to ensure all of the rice is coated.

Loosely cover the roasting pan with foil, then bake in the oven for 45–50 minutes until the coconut milk has been absorbed by the rice and the vegetables have softened.

Scatter with the spring onions and coriander, season with salt and lemon juice, then serve with more lemon wedges on the side.

Apple & ginger dhal

SERVES 2

• SUITABLE FOR FREEZING

200g (1 cup) dried split red lentils

1 large apple, coarsely grated

1 x 400ml (14fl oz) can full-fat coconut milk

1 rounded tbsp medium curry paste (ensure dairy-free)

pinch of dried chilli flakes, plus extra to serve

1cm (½in) piece of fresh ginger, finely grated

2 tbsp coconut yogurt

juice of ½ unwaxed lime, plus lime wedges to serve

small handful of coriander (cilantro) leaves, torn

generous pinch of sea salt

If you love dhal, but don't want to stand over the hob stirring a pan for 45 minutes, this will become your go-to recipe. Grated apple and ginger deliver the flavour to this lentil dish. Serve by itself or with rice for a hearty meal.

Preheat the oven to 200°C/400°F/gas mark 6.

Place the lentils and grated apple in a deep roasting pan.

In a jug, whisk together the coconut milk, curry paste, chilli flakes and grated ginger. Pour the mix over the lentils and apple.

Loosely cover the roasting pan with foil, then bake in the oven for 40–45 minutes until the lentils have softened.

Remove from the oven and discard the foil. Pour in 100ml (scant ½ cup) hot water and stir through until the lentils have broken down further, then season to taste with salt.

When ready to serve, divide between plates, top with the coconut yogurt, lime juice and coriander, then sprinkle with a few more dried chilli flakes, if you like.

EASY TIP:

Keep fresh ginger in the freezer, then simply grate from frozen into dhals, stir-fries and curries. This will reduce any waste, and keep the ginger fresh for when you need it.

Creamy massaman curry

with edamame

SERVES 4

• SUITABLE FOR FREEZING

1 x 400ml (14fl oz) can full-fat coconut milk

2 tbsp red Thai curry paste (ensure vegan)

1 rounded tbsp peanut butter

2 tbsp light soy sauce

2 tsp maple syrup

6 baby potatoes, halved

2 carrots, peeled and cut into matchsticks

½ butternut squash, peeled and chopped into bite-sized chunks

1 red (bell) pepper, thinly sliced

handful of sugarsnap peas, halved lengthways

handful of edamame beans (fresh or frozen)

1 cinnamon stick

1 bay leaf

2 spring onions (scallions), finely chopped

handful of coriander (cilantro) leaves, torn

1 small red chilli, deseeded and thinly sliced

2 tbsp salted peanuts, roughly chopped

wedges of unwaxed lime, to serve

This is my favourite way to make Thai-style massaman curry, as baking it in the oven results in a thick and creamy sauce with a velvety texture. Serve with fluffy coconut rice (page 121), quinoa or some plain basmati rice.

Preheat the oven to 200°C/400°F/gas mark 6.

In a bowl or jug (pitcher), whisk together the coconut milk, curry paste, peanut butter, soy sauce and maple syrup. Pour into a deep roasting pan.

Add the potatoes, carrots, butternut squash, red pepper, sugarsnap peas and edamame beans to the roasting pan, then tuck in the cinnamon stick and bay leaf. Cover the roasting pan loosely with foil, then bake in the oven for 30 minutes.

Carefully remove the foil, stir the curry and return to the oven for a further 30 minutes, uncovered, until the sauce has thickened and the potatoes are golden.

Remove from the oven and scatter with the spring onions, coriander, chilli and chopped peanuts. Serve with lime wedges.

EASY TIP:

This curry is gently spiced, but to make it milder, use just 1 tablespoon of red Thai curry paste and omit the sliced red chilli.

Orange, tofu & chilli noodles

SERVES 2

1 x 280g (9½oz) block of extra-firm tofu, drained and pressed (see Easy Tip) and cut into bite-sized cubes

drizzle of sunflower oil

1 tbsp light soy sauce

1 small red chilli, deseeded and thinly sliced

200g (7oz) Tenderstem broccoli

generous handful of sugarsnap peas, sliced diagonally

300g (10oz) ready-to-wok noodles (ensure egg-free)

zest and juice of ½ unwaxed orange

1 tsp sesame seeds

1 tsp roasted cashews

1 spring onion (scallion), finely chopped

small handful of coriander (cilantro) leaves, torn

Put the wok away and throw the ingredients into a roasting pan! Crispy baked tofu, broccoli, cashews and soft noodles are baked with orange and soy. Ready-to-wok noodles can be found in supermarkets, but check that they do not contain eggs.

Preheat the oven to 200°C/400°F/gas mark 6.

Place the tofu in a deep roasting pan and drizzle with the sunflower oil and soy sauce. Bake in the oven for 20 minutes, then remove from the oven and use tongs to turn the tofu. Throw in the chilli, broccoli and sugarsnap peas and cook for a further 10 minutes.

Meanwhile, soak the noodles in hot water for a couple of minutes, until they are easy to separate. Drain away the hot water.

Add the noodles to the pan, tucking them in around the tofu and vegetables, then scatter over the orange zest and squeeze over the juice, followed by the sesame seeds and cashews. Return to the oven for 5–6 minutes until the noodles are hot.

Remove from the oven and scatter over the spring onion and coriander leaves.

EASY TIP:

The key to cooking perfect extra-firm tofu is to remove as much moisture as possible, by draining and pressing the block of tofu. You can purchase a tofu press to do this effectively, or simply wrap the tofu in kitchen paper or a clean, dry tea (dish) towel and place on a large plate. Place another plate on top of the block and add a couple of cookbooks or a heavy pan to weigh it down. Allow to stand for 1 hour, before slicing the tofu into the desired pieces.

Easiest-ever pulled jackfruit buns

with coleslaw

SERVES 2

1 x 400g (14oz) can jackfruit, drained and rinsed

6 rounded tbsp barbecue sauce (ensure vegan)

small handful of flat-leaf parsley, roughly chopped

¼ red cabbage, very thinly sliced

1 carrot, peeled and grated

2 spring onions (scallions), thinly sliced

small handful of sultanas (golden raisins)

2 tbsp vegan mayonnaise

juice of ¼ unwaxed lemon

2 burger buns (ensure vegan), halved

generous pinch of sea salt and black pepper

Let the oven do the hard work with this sticky pulled jackfruit that is perfect loaded into a warmed burger bun, toasted pitta bread or flatbread. Canned jackfruit can be found in most large supermarkets, and has a meaty 'pulled' texture, especially when baked with barbecue sauce.

Preheat the oven to 180°C/350°F/gas mark 4.

Add the jackfruit to a large bowl and break into rough shreds. Stir in the barbecue sauce and chopped parsley until all of the jackfruit is coated, then spoon into a roasting pan. Bake in the oven for 20–25 minutes until the jackfruit is sticky.

Meanwhile, stir together the cabbage, carrot, spring onions and sultanas in a bowl, then mix in the vegan mayonnaise and lemon juice.

Warm the burger buns in the oven for a couple of minutes. Remove the buns and the pulled jackfruit. Season the jackfruit to taste with salt and pepper.

Load the pulled jackfruit into the warmed buns, then spoon in the coleslaw. Serve hot.

EASY TIP:

This simple coleslaw can be thrown together in the time that it takes for the jackfruit to cook in the oven. If there's coleslaw left over, it will keep in the fridge for up to 3 days for use on jacket potatoes or salads.

Oven-fried nuggets

with a cornflake crust

SERVES 2

8 rounded tbsp cornflakes (ensure vegan, see Easy Tip)

generous pinch of sea salt and black pepper

4 rounded tbsp sweet chilli sauce

drizzle of sunflower oil

1 x 280g (9½oz) block of extra-firm tofu, drained and pressed (see Easy Tip on page 68)

Bake these spicy tofu nuggets in less than 30 minutes! Tender tofu is coated with sweet chilli sauce then covered in crispy cornflakes, for a simple and delicious treat! Serve with skin-on potato wedges (page 117) and tomato ketchup.

Preheat the oven to 190°C/375°F/gas mark 5.

Spoon the cornflakes into a jug blender or food processor and blitz until a fine breadcrumb is created. Pour onto a plate and season with salt and plenty of pepper.

In a bowl, stir together the sweet chilli sauce and sunflower oil.

Slice the pressed tofu block horizontally into 3 slices, then cut each slice into 2cm (¾in) fingers. Dip each finger of tofu into the sweet chilli mix, then roll it into the cornflake breadcrumbs. Place on a baking sheet and repeat with the remaining fingers of tofu.

Bake in the oven for 25 minutes until crisp. Serve hot.

EASY TIPS:

Some brands of cornflakes contain vitamin D obtained from sheep's wool, making the product unsuitable for vegans. Many supermarket own-brands do not fortify using this source of vitamin D, or consider cornflake brands found in the free-from aisle of your local supermarket as many of these will be labelled as vegan.

This recipe is easy to scale up if you're having friends over, just double or triple the ingredients. You may have to cook them in batches depending on how many baking sheets you have!

Pizza-loaded potato skins

SERVES 4

4 large baking potatoes, scrubbed clean and thoroughly dried

1 tbsp sunflower oil

4 rounded tbsp vegan cream cheese

handful of pitted black olives, roughly sliced

4 sundried tomatoes in oil, drained and roughly chopped

pinch of dried oregano

2 large tomatoes, each thinly sliced into 8 rounds

generous pinch of sea salt and black pepper

small handful of basil leaves

Looking for the perfect Friday night feast? These pizza-loaded potato skins are full of flavour and are perfect to eat while binge-watching that box set! Use this as a base recipe and add your favourite pizza toppings, including sweetcorn, chopped artichokes or pineapple.

EASY TIP:

Get ahead by baking the jacket potatoes up to a day in advance, then prepare the filling fresh before enjoying.

Preheat the oven to 200°C/400°F/gas mark 6.

Pierce the potatoes with a fork a few times, then rub with the sunflower oil. Wrap each potato in foil, then place in a roasting pan. Bake in the oven for 1½ hours until softened.

Remove from the oven and carefully fold back the foil. Halve each potato and leave until cool enough to comfortably handle. When cool enough, carefully scoop out the potato flesh from each half into a bowl, leaving about 5mm (¼in) of potato remaining near the skin.

Mash the potato in the bowl, along with the vegan cream cheese. Stir in the olives, sundried tomatoes and oregano, then load each potato skin with the filling. Lay a slice of tomato over each potato half.

Bake in the oven for 20 minutes until the filling is golden and bubbling.

Remove from the oven and season with salt and pepper. Scatter a couple of basil leaves over each potato half before serving.

Baked sweet potato chilli

SERVES 4

• SUITABLE FOR FREEZING

1 x 400g (14oz) can chopped tomatoes

1 tbsp tomato purée (paste)

1 rounded tsp mild chilli powder

1 tsp smoked paprika

¼ tsp dried oregano

pinch of ground cinnamon

2 sweet potatoes, peeled and cut into 2cm (¾in) cubes

1 yellow (bell) pepper, roughly diced

1 celery stick, finely diced

1 x 400g (14oz) can red kidney beans, drained and rinsed

1 avocado, peeled, stoned and sliced

juice of ½ unwaxed lime

pinch of smoked sea salt

handful of coriander (cilantro) leaves, roughly torn

Midweek meals should be easy to prepare, comforting, and enjoyed by the whole family. This chilli requires no standing over a pan stirring, just sit back and let the oven do all the hard work! I often cook this chilli in a lidded cast-iron casserole dish, for an oven-to-table dinner. Serve with skin-on potato wedges (page 117).

Preheat the oven to 200°C/400°F/gas mark 6.

In a deep roasting pan, whisk together the chopped tomatoes, tomato purée, chilli powder, smoked paprika, oregano and cinnamon until combined.

Stir in the sweet potato, yellow pepper, celery and red kidney beans, then cover with foil.

Bake in the oven for 35–40 minutes until the sweet potato has softened. Carefully remove from the oven and discard the foil. Layer over the avocado slices and squeeze over the lime juice. Season with smoked sea salt and scatter with coriander leaves.

EASY TIP:

A pinch of ground cinnamon balances the smoky flavour of the chilli, while working perfectly with the sweet potato. You'll never look back once you've tried it!

Creamy roasted mushrooms

with thyme & white beans

1 garlic clove, halved

200g (7oz) baby button mushrooms, brushed clean

drizzle of sunflower oil

250ml (1 cup) soya single (light) cream

1 sprig of fresh thyme

1 x 400g (14oz) can cannellini beans, drained and rinsed

generous pinch of sea salt and black pepper

small handful of flat-leaf parsley, finely chopped

SERVES 2 GENEROUSLY

Earthy mushrooms are roasted until fragrant, then baked in a thyme-scented cream. This simple supper is comforting, warming and satisfying. Serve on toasted sourdough.

Preheat the oven to 200°C/400°F/gas mark 6.

Rub the garlic clove over the surface of a deep roasting pan to release the fragrance, then discard it. Add the mushrooms to the pan, drizzle with sunflower oil, then roast in the oven for 15 minutes.

Carefully remove the roasting pan from the oven and pour in the soya cream. Lay in the sprig of thyme and stir in the cannellini beans. Loosely cover the pan with foil, then return to the oven for 20 minutes.

Remove from the oven and season generously with salt and pepper. Scatter with the flat-leaf parsley just before serving.

EASY TIP:

If you happen to have some left over, simply discard the thyme sprig, then blend with vegetable stock to make a fragrant soup for the following day.

Sausages with apples & blackberries

6 Lincolnshire-style vegan sausages

6 baby potatoes, quartered

2 small apples, halved

generous handful of blackberries

1 small red onion, finely chopped

pinch of dried sage

drizzle of sunflower oil

generous pinch of sea salt and black pepper

SERVES 2

This recipe is both easy and comforting, making it perfect for those blustery autumn evenings. I love to use herby Lincolnshire-style vegan sausages, but feel free to use your own favourites. Serve this on its own, or as part of your Sunday roast dinner.

Preheat the oven to 200°C/400°F/gas mark 6.

Lay the sausages, potatoes, apple, blackberries and red onion in a roasting pan.

Scatter with sage and drizzle with sunflower oil, then loosely cover with foil.

Bake in the oven for 20 minutes, then carefully remove the foil and bake for a further 10 minutes until the tops of the sausages are golden.

Remove from the oven and season with a generous pinch of salt and pepper before serving.

EASY TIP:
Switch the apple for pear, thin wedges of pumpkin, or plums, for easy flavour variations.

Toad in the hole pie

SERVES 4

8 frozen vegan sausages

2 small red onions, peeled and quartered

drizzle of sunflower oil

1 sheet of shop-bought puff pastry (ensure dairy-free)

generous pinch of dried sage

generous pinch of sea salt and black pepper

This is a simple hybrid version of toad in the hole and a puff-pastry pie – what could be any better? Whether you serve this hearty meal midweek or as part of a Sunday roast, it is set to be a real crowd pleaser. Serve with lashings of vegan gravy and steamed greens, if you like.

EASY TIP:
Many brands of shop-bought puff pastry are suitable for vegans as vegetable oil is used instead of dairy butter, but always read the ingredients before purchasing.

Preheat the oven to 200°C/400°F/gas mark 6.

Arrange the frozen sausages in a roasting pan along with the red onions. Drizzle with a little sunflower oil and bake in the oven for half of the recommended cooking time of the sausages (see the manufacturer's cooking instructions on the pack), which will be approximately 10–15 minutes.

Remove from the oven, transfer the sausages and onion to a plate for a moment, and allow the roasting pan to cool for a few minutes. Keep the oven on.

Line the roasting pan with baking parchment. Lay in the sheet of puff pastry and fold over the edges by 1cm, pressing down slightly. Evenly place the sausages on the pastry, then use a knife to lightly score the pastry around each sausage. Scatter over the roasted onion and sprinkle with sage.

Bake the pie for 12–15 minutes, until golden and risen. Remove from the oven and season to taste with sea salt and black pepper.

Puttanesca pasta bake

SERVES 2

200g (7oz) dried penne pasta (ensure egg-free)

500g (2 cups) passata

pinch of sugar

1 garlic clove, very thinly sliced

pinch of dried chilli flakes

handful of pitted black olives, sliced

1 heaped tsp capers, drained

4 sundried tomatoes, drained of oil and roughly chopped

2 tbsp grated vegan hard cheese

generous pinch of black pepper

small handful of basil leaves

This is a non-traditional way of cooking pasta alla puttanesca, but who can resist an all-in-one pasta bake? There's no need to pre-cook the pasta, but a simple soak in hot water will ensure it is al dente at the end of cooking, as well as making the pasta sauce extra silky.

Preheat the oven to 180°C/350°F/gas mark 4.

Put the pasta into a heatproof bowl and pour over enough boiling water to cover it. Allow to stand for 5 minutes, then drain away the water.

Combine the passata, sugar, garlic, chilli flakes, olives, capers and sundried tomatoes with 100ml (scant ½ cup) water in the base of a deep roasting pan.

Tip the pasta into the pan and stir to combine fully. Cover loosely with foil, then bake in the oven for 40 minutes.

Carefully remove from the oven and discard the foil. Scatter over the cheese and return to the oven for 5 minutes.

Remove from the oven and season with pepper, then scatter with basil leaves just before serving.

EASY TIP:

Use your favourite pasta in this dish. I've been known to use half penne and half fusilli, just to use up the odds and ends left in the cupboard!

Courgette rotolo

with cream cheese & spinach in a marinara sauce

SERVES 2 GENEROUSLY

500g (2 cups) passata

1 garlic clove, very thinly sliced

generous handful of basil leaves, finely chopped

small handful of flat-leaf parsley, finely chopped

generous pinch of sea salt and black pepper

2 large courgettes (zucchini), very thinly sliced into ribbons (see Easy Tip)

4 heaped tbsp vegan cream cheese

drizzle of extra virgin olive oil

handful of baby spinach leaves, roughly chopped

small handful of fresh chives, finely chopped

This supper is elegant enough to be served for dinner guests, but simple enough to enjoy midweek with the family. Use your favourite vegan cream cheese (found in most supermarkets) to make the rich rotolo filling.

Preheat the oven to 180°C/350°F/gas mark 4.

Stir together the passata, garlic, basil and parsley in the bottom of a deep roasting pan. Season with a pinch of sea salt and black pepper, then cover the pan with foil and bake in the oven for 30 minutes.

Meanwhile, lay the thin courgette slices between kitchen paper or a clean tea (dish) towel for 15 minutes to absorb some of the excess moisture.

In a bowl, stir together the cream cheese, olive oil, spinach and chives. Spread one side of each courgette strip with the cream cheese mixture using the back of a teaspoon.

Remove the roasting pan from the oven and discard the foil. Roll each courgette slice up, then carefully place in the hot sauce.

Return the roasting pan to the oven for a further 30 minutes, then season with a pinch of salt and pepper before serving.

EASY TIP:

The slices of courgette need to be thin enough to roll. I use a Y-peeler or a mandoline to achieve this, as using a knife won't get the slices thin enough.

Mediterranean gnocchi bake

SERVES 2 GENEROUSLY

• SUITABLE FOR FREEZING

500g (2 cups) passata

generous handful of basil leaves, finely chopped (reserve a few small leaves to garnish)

1 garlic clove, very thinly sliced

1 yellow (bell) pepper, roughly sliced

1 courgette (zucchini), roughly chopped

8 cherry tomatoes, halved

500g (1lb 2oz) potato gnocchi (ensure egg-free), rinsed with hot water

6 tsp vegan cream cheese, chilled

generous pinch of sea salt and black pepper

drizzle of extra virgin olive oil

Dig into this hearty gnocchi one-pot for a summery yet substantial supper. I love the mild and creamy finish from the vegan cream cheese spooned over. Serve with crusty bread or garlic bread, if you like.

Preheat the oven to 200°C/400°F/gas mark 6.

Stir together the passata, chopped basil and garlic in the bottom of a deep roasting pan, then add the pepper, courgette and cherry tomatoes.

Add the rinsed gnocchi and cover the pan loosely with foil. Bake in the oven for 30–35 minutes until the gnocchi have become tender.

Remove the pan from the oven and discard the foil. Dollop over the cream cheese in teaspoon-sized amounts, pressing them gently into the sauce. Scatter over the reserved basil leaves and season with salt and pepper. Drizzle over a little olive oil and serve hot.

EASY TIP:

Shop-bought gnocchi is a store cupboard essential, and perfect for cooking up a substantial meal when you fancy an alternative to pasta. Experiment with flavoured varieties including pumpkin or spinach, but do ensure they are egg-free.

Roasted ratatouille

SERVES 2 GENEROUSLY

• SUITABLE FOR FREEZING

1 tbsp sunflower oil

1 x 400g (14oz) can chopped tomatoes

1 tbsp tomato purée (paste)

1 tsp dried oregano

½ tsp dried mixed herbs

4 beef tomatoes, sliced 1cm (½in) thick

1 large red onion, sliced 1cm (½in) thick

1 large courgette (zucchini), sliced 1cm (½in) thick

1 large aubergine (eggplant), sliced 1cm (½in) thick

pinch of sea salt and black pepper

handful of small basil leaves

Everyone loves this fresh classic, especially when it is so easy to make. It looks beautiful served at the dinner table too! Serve with crusty bread and vegan butter, and a glass of red wine, if you like.

Preheat the oven to 180°C/350°F/gas mark 4.

Stir together the oil, chopped tomatoes, tomato purée, oregano and mixed herbs in the bottom of a small but deep roasting pan.

Arrange the sliced tomatoes, red onion, courgette and aubergine in rows in the roasting pan, alternating the colours as you go.

Bake in the oven for 1 hour until the vegetables have softened and the edges are golden, then top with fresh basil before serving.

EASY TIP:

To serve more people, or to add extra substance, pour in 400g (14oz) drained and rinsed canned cannellini beans with the chopped tomatoes.

Harissa falafel bake

SERVES 2 GENEROUSLY

500g (2 cups) passata

2 tsp harissa paste

1 yellow (bell) pepper, thinly sliced

1 small red onion, thinly sliced

1 small courgette (zucchini), thinly sliced into half-moons

8 shop-bought falafel (ensure vegan)

generous pinch of sea salt and black pepper

small handful of flat-leaf parsley, finely chopped

drizzle of good-quality tahini

This gently spiced bake has a cook time of 30 minutes, with very little pre-preparation. To save time, feel free to slice the pepper, onion and courgette up to a day in advance, and keep refrigerated and covered. Serve hot with toasted pitta breads and houmous.

Preheat the oven to 200°C/400°F/gas mark 6.

Pour the passata into a deep roasting pan and swirl in the harissa. Add the sliced pepper, red onion and courgette and cover the pan loosely with foil. Bake in the oven for 15 minutes.

Carefully remove the pan from the oven and discard the foil. Add the falafel and return to the oven for 15 minutes until the falafel have become golden on top.

Remove from the oven and season with salt and pepper. Scatter over the chopped parsley and drizzle with tahini.

EASY TIP:

Shop-bought falafel are a handy item to have in the fridge or freezer, for quick lunches, speedy snacks and this delicious supper. If you find them a little dry or crumbly, simply drizzle with extra virgin olive oil. Ensure they do not contain eggs or dairy, as these can sometimes be added to shop-bought varieties.

Moroccan-style bake

SERVES 4

• SUITABLE FOR FREEZING

2 generous tbsp sunflower oil

1 tsp harissa paste

1 tsp ground cumin

¼ tsp ground turmeric

1 small butternut squash, deseeded and cut into bite-sized cubes

1 sweet potato, peeled and cut into bite-sized chunks

2 small red onions, peeled and quartered

1 carrot, peeled and sliced into rounds

handful of dried apricots

1 unwaxed lemon, quartered

1 x 400g (14oz) can chickpeas (garbanzo beans), drained and rinsed

small handful of flat-leaf parsley

seeds of ½ pomegranate

1 tbsp shelled pistachios, roughly chopped

generous pinch of sea salt

Spices, herbs, root vegetables and pomegranate come together in this flavoursome bake. I love this combination of vegetables for a hearty supper, but you can also switch it up with aubergine, cauliflower and cherry tomatoes. Serve with couscous and a spoonful of plain soya yogurt.

Preheat the oven to 180°C/350°F/gas mark 4.

In a deep roasting pan, whisk together the oil, harissa, cumin and turmeric. Tip in the butternut squash, sweet potato, onions, carrot and apricots and toss to coat in the oil. Add the quartered lemon, then roast in the oven for 30 minutes.

Carefully remove the roasting pan from the oven and tip in the chickpeas, then return to the oven for a further 10 minutes.

Remove the roasting pan from the oven and scatter with the parsley, pomegranate seeds and pistachios. Season to taste with salt, then serve.

Pictured overleaf

EASY TIP:

Use the remaining half of the pomegranate for my chickpea and olive orzo bake (page 92).

Moroccan-
style bake

Chickpea & olive orzo

SERVES 2 GENEROUSLY

• SUITABLE FOR FREEZING

500g (2 cups) passata

1 tbsp rose harissa paste

1 tsp dried oregano

pinch of ground cinnamon

4 tbsp dried orzo pasta (ensure egg-free)

1 x 400g (14oz) can chickpeas (garbanzo beans), drained and rinsed

handful of pitted green olives

juice of ¼ unwaxed lemon

generous pinch of sea salt

small handful of flat-leaf parsley, finely chopped

seeds of ½ pomegranate

2 tbsp plain soya yogurt

Gentle heat, pops of fruity pomegranate, savoury olives and nutty chickpeas – this bake is substantial and nutritious, with very little preparation needed! Delicious and comforting bowl-food.

Preheat the oven to 200°C/400°F/gas mark 6.

Whisk together the passata, harissa, oregano and cinnamon in the bottom of a roasting pan, then stir in the orzo and chickpeas.

Cover the pan loosely with foil, then bake in the oven for 30 minutes. Discard the foil and scatter in the olives, then return to the oven for a further 20 minutes until the orzo is plump.

Remove the roasting pan from the oven and squeeze over the lemon juice. Season with a little sea salt, then scatter over the flat-leaf parsley and pomegranate seeds. Spoon over the soya yogurt just before serving.

EASY TIP:

Orzo is small, rice-shaped pasta. Many dried varieties are egg-free and vegan-friendly, but always check the ingredients before purchasing.

Extras

Slow-roasted garlic

2 large bulbs of garlic

drizzle of olive oil

small handful of flat-leaf parsley, very finely chopped

pinch of sea salt

SERVES 4 GENEROUSLY

• SUITABLE FOR FREEZING

There's nothing more divine than roasted garlic spread onto warm, crusty bread – I like to have this for lunch or a snack, or serve it alongside salady suppers. You can also mix it into vegan mayonnaise for a delicious garlic mayo.

Preheat the oven to 120°C/250°F/gas mark ½.

Place the bulbs on a baking sheet and drizzle with olive oil.

Roast in the oven for 3 hours, then remove and allow to cool until the garlic is cool enough to handle.

Snip the tops off the bulbs, then squeeze the soft, roasted garlic out of each clove into a small bowl and discard the skins. Use a fork to gently mash the softened garlic until smooth. Stir in the parsley and salt and drizzle in a little extra olive oil. Keep in the fridge and serve within 2 days.

EASY TIP:

This recipe requires the same roasting time and oven temperature as 3-hour roasted tomatoes (page 99), so cook at the same time to save energy and effort.

Black pepper croutons

2 thick slices of slightly stale bread, cut into even cubes

2 tsp sunflower oil

generous pinch of sea salt snd black pepper

SERVES 4

Croutons are not just for topping soup! Toss into my warm peach and basil salad (page 20), serve as part of a cooked breakfast as a lighter alternative to fried bread, or dip into houmous.

Preheat the oven to 180°C/350°F/gas mark 4.

Lay the cubes of bread on a baking sheet and drizzle with olive oil. Generously scatter with salt and pepper, then bake in the oven for 8–10 minutes until golden and crunchy.

EASY TIP:

These croutons will last for up to 3 days in a sealed container, if allowed to cool completely after baking.

3-hour roasted tomatoes

300g (10oz) baby plum tomatoes, halved

drizzle of olive oil

generous pinch of sea salt and black pepper

SERVES 4

• SUITABLE FOR FREEZING

These semi-dried tomatoes make a perfect toast-topper, a flavoursome addition to a salad, or are delicious simply served with olives, crusty bread and balsamic vinegar.

Preheat the oven to 120°C/250°F/gas mark ½.

Place the tomato halves in a single layer in a roasting pan, cut side up. Drizzle with olive oil, then roast in the oven for 3 hours until the skins have become wrinkled.

Remove from the oven and season with salt and pepper.

Pictured overleaf

EASY TIP:

Baby plum tomatoes have a sweet and rich flavour when roasted, but experiment with other varieties, including small heritage tomatoes of mixed colours.

3-hour
roasted
tomatoes

Cherry tomato & balsamic bruschetta

SERVES 4

300g (10oz) cherry tomatoes, ideally on the vine

½ red onion, thinly sliced into half rings

2 tbsp good-quality balsamic vinegar

drizzle of olive oil, plus extra to finish

1 small baguette, cut in half then cut horizontally in half again

handful of basil leaves

generous pinch of sea salt and black pepper

Glaze roasted cherry tomatoes and red onion with balsamic vinegar for a tangy twist on this Italian favourite. Serve as a starter or lunch, or enjoy as a snack.

Preheat the oven to 200°C/400°F/gas mark 6.

Place the cherry tomatoes and sliced red onion in a roasting pan and drizzle with the balsamic vinegar and olive oil. Roast in the oven for 15 minutes until the tomatoes have started to blister a little and the onion is softened.

Place the baguette pieces in the oven and warm for 5 minutes while the tomatoes and onion finish cooking.

Remove the warm bread from the oven and place on serving plates. Load the hot tomatoes and onions onto the bread and scatter with basil leaves. Season with salt and pepper.

EASY TIP:

These bruschetta can be enjoyed hot or cold. If enjoying cold, simply cook the balsamic tomatoes and onions, then cool to room temperature before enjoying fresh that day.

Crispy chilli & lime chickpeas

SERVES 2 GENEROUSLY AS A SNACK

1 x 400g (14oz) can chickpeas (garbanzo beans), drained and rinsed

2 tbsp sunflower oil

1½ tsp smoked paprika

½ tsp mild chilli powder

pinch of dried oregano

pinch of soft light brown sugar

generous pinch of sea salt

finely grated zest of ½ unwaxed lime

If the snack supplies are looking depleted – don't panic, these crispy snacks will save the day using store-cupboard ingredients! Perfect for lunchboxes, for both adults and children.

Preheat the oven to 200°C/400°F/gas mark 6.

Pour the rinsed chickpeas onto a clean, dry tea (dish) towel or some kitchen paper and blot away as much moisture as possible. Be firm while doing this, for the outer shell of the chickpeas to peel away and the snacks to become crunchier.

Tip the chickpeas into a roasting pan and stir in the sunflower oil. Spoon in the smoked paprika, chilli powder, oregano, brown sugar and sea salt and stir to coat the chickpeas. Stir through the lime zest, then bake in the oven for 15 minutes.

Carefully shake the pan to turn the chickpeas, then return to the oven for a further 15–18 minutes until the chickpeas are crisp. Allow to cool a little, then serve warm or at room temperature.

EASY TIP:
Store these snacks in a sealed container to retain optimum crunch.

Spiced cavolo nero crisps

SERVES 2 GENEROUSLY

2 tsp sunflower oil

1 tsp light soy sauce

pinch of Chinese five-spice

pinch of dried chilli flakes

4 large leaves of cavolo nero, tough stems removed and leaves torn into 4cm (1½in) pieces

Cavolo nero is the dark and leafy cousin to kale, with a rich flavour and satisfying texture. Delicious as a snack, used as a crispy soup topping, or as a side dish to any Chinese-style meal.

Preheat the oven to 180°C/350°F/gas mark 4.

In a bowl, stir together the sunflower oil, soy sauce, Chinese five-spice and chilli flakes.

Stir in the cavolo nero and coat evenly with the oil and spice mix. Shake off any excess oil, then place the cavolo nero on a baking sheet. Bake in the oven for 10–12 minutes until crispy.

EASY TIP:

These crisps can be served warm or cold, and will last for up to 2 days in a sealed container.

Za'atar pitta chips

SERVES 2 GENEROUSLY

2 white pitta breads, sliced into even triangles

1 tbsp sunflower oil

¼ tsp za'atar

pinch of dried chilli flakes

pinch of sea salt

Dip these crunchy chips into your favourite houmous, or enjoy as a lunchbox snack. Za'atar is a Middle Eastern spice blend, which can be found in most large supermarkets. Eat these pitta chips fresh, or store in a sealed contained for up to 3 days.

Preheat the oven to 180°C/350°F/gas mark 4.

Place the pitta triangles on a baking sheet, then use a pastry brush to lightly cover both sides with the oil.

Sprinkle over the za'atar and chilli flakes, then bake in the oven for 8–10 minutes until golden and crisp.

Remove from the oven and sprinkle with sea salt. Serve warm or allow to cool to room temperature.

Pictured overleaf

EASY TIP:

This is the perfect way to use up those last pitta breads in the packet, even if they are turning stale.

Carrot & maple dip

SERVES 4 GENEROUSLY

• SUITABLE FOR FREEZING

300g (10oz) carrots, peeled and roughly chopped into small pieces

drizzle of sunflower oil

2 tbsp maple syrup

pinch of dried chilli flakes

juice of ½ unwaxed lemon

small handful of coriander (cilantro) leaves, finely chopped

generous pinch of sea salt

For a fresher, lighter alternative to houmous, whip up this roasted carrot dip. Maple, chilli and lemon brighten up humble carrots, for an easy-to-prepare dip to share. Serve with za'atar pitta chips (opposite).

Preheat the oven to 200°C/400°F/gas mark 6.

Arrange the carrots in a roasting pan and drizzle with sunflower oil. Drizzle over the maple syrup and scatter with chilli flakes.

Roast in the oven for 18–20 minutes until the carrots are soft, then carefully remove the roasting pan from the oven.

Allow the carrots to cool a little, then spoon into a bowl. Squeeze over the lemon juice then use a fork to mash until semi-smooth. Stir in the chopped coriander and season to taste with salt.

Pictured overleaf

EASY TIP:

I love this dip left a little chunky, for a rustic texture. If you prefer a smooth dip, simply blitz the roasted carrots in a blender with the lemon juice, then stir through the coriander and sea salt.

Za'atar pitta chips
with carrot &
maple dip

Fennel seed crackers

SERVES 4

150g (1¼ cups) plain (all-purpose) flour, plus extra for dusting

1 tsp sea salt

½ tsp soft light brown sugar

1 heaped tsp fennel seeds

2 tbsp sunflower oil

These crispy crackers are simple to make with store cupboard ingredients – perfect as a snack whenever the mood arises. Use this as a basic recipe for many more cracker variations by switching the fennel seeds for finely chopped fresh sage, rosemary or cracked black pepper. Serve with slow-roasted garlic (page 96) and a slice of vegan cheese.

Preheat the oven to 200°C/400°F/gas mark 6 and line a baking sheet with baking parchment.

In a bowl, stir together the flour, salt, sugar and fennel seeds until combined. Make a well in the middle of the bowl and pour in the oil with 80ml (⅓ cup) water, then stir until a smooth dough forms.

Sprinkle a clean work surface with about 1 tablespoon flour and roll out the dough to 5mm (¼in) thick. Slice the dough into small squares and place them on the lined baking sheet, with a gap between each one to allow for some spreading of the dough. Alternatively, transfer the whole sheet of dough to the baking sheet without slicing (as pictured).

Bake in the oven for 13–15 minutes until just golden, then remove from the oven and allow to cool fully to become extra crisp. If you've baked your crackers in one large sheet you can break it apart once cool.

EASY TIP:

Use a pizza cutter to cut the dough into squares instead of a knife, for an easier way to slice.

Roasted radishes with parsley butter

200g (7oz) radishes, halved or left whole

drizzle of sunflower oil

1 tbsp vegan butter

small handful of flat-leaf parsley, finely chopped

generous pinch of sea salt and black pepper

SERVES 2

Raw radishes have a feisty, peppery flavour and crunchy texture, but roast them in the oven and magic will happen! Sharp flavours are replaced with a sweet, mellow taste. Serve warm with fresh salad leaves, or as an unexpected vegetable with your Sunday roast dinner.

Preheat the oven to 180°C/350°F/gas mark 4.

Arrange the radishes in a roasting pan and drizzle with sunflower oil.

Roast in the oven for 20 minutes, then carefully remove the roasting pan from the oven. Swirl the vegan butter between the radishes and scatter in the chopped parsley. Return to the oven for 5 minutes until the butter has melted.

Remove from the oven and season generously with salt and pepper.

EASY TIP:
This recipe is easy to double up when serving more guests.

Skin-on potato wedges

SERVES 4

4 large baking potatoes, scrubbed clean and sliced into even wedges

1 tbsp sunflower oil

1 tsp Cajun seasoning

pinch of smoked paprika

generous pinch of sea salt

Rustic, skin-on potato wedges are the ultimate side dish, perfect served with delicious roasted mushroom burgers (page 60) or as a comforting late-night snack.

Preheat the oven to 200°C/400°F/gas mark 6.

Place the potato wedges in a large roasting pan and stir through the sunflower oil, Cajun seasoning and smoked paprika until evenly coated.

Bake in the oven for 30–35 minutes until golden. Sprinkle with sea salt before serving.

EASY TIP:

Cajun seasoning can be found in large supermarkets, or substitute with mild chilli powder and a pinch of dried thyme.

Baked corn on the cob

SERVES 6

6 rounded tsp vegan butter

1 large garlic clove, crushed

small handful of flat-leaf parsley, finely chopped

zest of ½ unwaxed lemon

generous pinch of sea salt

6 corn on the cobs

There's something about the fresh, sweet, buttery flavour of corn on the cob that makes it the perfect comfort food for any season. Wrap these cobs in foil before oven baking, for a fuss-free way of enjoying these moreish delights.

Preheat the oven to 200°C/400°F/gas mark 6.

In a small bowl, stir together the vegan butter, garlic, parsley, lemon zest and sea salt.

Cut 6 pieces of kitchen foil, large enough to wrap around a cob, then place a corn cob in the centre of each. Spread most of the butter mix evenly onto each cob, reserving some for later, then wrap the foil securely.

Place the foiled cobs in a roasting pan, then bake in the oven for 30–35 minutes until tender.

Fold back the foil, then place the under a hot grill (broiler) for a minute or two until slightly charred. Slather with the remaining butter and serve.

EASY TIP:

The garlic, lemon and herb butter can be made up to 2 days in advance when kept in the fridge.

Sticky baked tofu

SERVES 4

3 heaped tbsp orange marmalade

2 tbsp light soy sauce

1 tbsp sunflower oil

pinch of dried chilli flakes

1 x 390g (14oz) block of extra-firm tofu, drained and pressed (see Easy Tip on page 68)

½ tsp sesame seeds

2 spring onions (scallions), thinly sliced

small handful of coriander (cilantro) leaves, roughly torn

Baked instead of fried, this tasty tofu is easy to prepare and delicious to eat! Serve as a side dish to any Chinese-style feast, or with basmati rice for a simple supper.

Preheat the oven to 180°C/350°F/gas mark 4.

In a bowl, whisk together the marmalade, soy sauce, sunflower oil and chilli flakes.

Slice through the tofu lengthways to create 3 thin blocks of tofu. Then chop each slice into even triangles.

Dip each triangle of tofu into the marmalade mixture to generously coat. Place the coated tofu in a roasting pan. Bake in the oven for 35–40 minutes, until the sticky coating appears to have reduced.

Remove from the oven and scatter with sesame seeds, spring onions and coriander.

EASY TIP:

The sticky glaze can be made up to 2 days in advance when kept in the fridge.

Fluffy coconut rice

500g (2½ cups) white basmati rice

2 tbsp desiccated (dried shredded) coconut

1 x 400ml (14fl oz) can coconut milk

pinch of sea salt

SERVES 4 AS A SIDE

• SUITABLE FOR FREEZING

If cooking up the perfect pan of rice remains a challenge, allow your oven to do all of the hard work! Covering the dish with foil allows steam to circulate and create the fluffiest rice.

Preheat the oven to 180°C/350°F/gas mark 4.

Pour the rice and desiccated coconut into a deep roasting pan.

Pour in the coconut milk, along with 600ml (2½ cups) hot water. Stir to distribute, then cover the pan with foil.

Bake in the oven for 30–35 minutes until the rice is plump and fluffy. Season with salt to taste.

EASY TIP:

For pilau rice, add 1 litre (4 cups) of hot water instead of coconut milk, and throw in a cinnamon stick, 2 bay leaves and ½ teaspoon of ground turmeric.

Stuffed cabbage rolls

SERVES 4 AS A SIDE

200g (7oz) pre-cooked basmati rice (see Easy Tip)

30g (1oz) mint leaves, finely chopped

generous handful of fresh dill, finely chopped

generous handful of flat-leaf parsley, finely chopped

handful of fresh chives, finely chopped

juice of 1 unwaxed lemon

drizzle of extra virgin olive oil

generous pinch of sea salt

8–10 savoy cabbage leaves, tough lower stems removed

This simple side dish is fragrant, fresh and filling. Delicious served as part of a Middle Eastern-style feast, or as individual snacks. Keep refrigerated for up to 2 days.

Preheat the oven to 180°C/350°F/gas mark 4.

Spoon the rice into a large bowl and stir through the chopped mint, dill, parsley and chives. Stir in the lemon juice and olive oil until combined with the rice and herbs. Season to taste with salt.

Lay out a cabbage leaf in front of you. Spoon a heaped tablespoon of the herbed rice into the centre of the leaf, then fold the long sides inwards to meet in the centre. Then start rolling neatly from a short side until you form a sealed parcel. Place the stuffed leaf in a roasting dish, seam-side down, then repeat until you've filled all of the leaves. The stuffed leaves should be packed tightly next to each other in the roasting dish. Pour over 200ml (generous ¾ cup) boiling water, cover loosely with foil, then place in the oven for 30 minutes.

Carefully remove from the oven and allow to stand for a few minutes before serving.

EASY TIP:

Use a pre-cooked rice pouch available from supermarkets, or simply cook 100g (3½oz) white basmati rice in a pan of simmering water for 10–12 minutes, then allow the rice to cool before using to avoid it becoming sticky when baked. This is also a great recipe for using up leftover rice.

Bombay potatoes

SERVES 4 AS A SIDE

• SUITABLE FOR FREEZING

1 x 400g (14oz) can chopped tomatoes

1 tbsp mild curry paste (ensure dairy-free)

pinch of ground turmeric

pinch of ground cumin

1 red chilli, deseeded and thinly sliced

700g (1½lb) new potatoes, halved or quartered

200g (7oz) cherry tomatoes

handful of coriander (cilantro) leaves, roughly torn

generous pinch of sea salt and black pepper

Fragrant, spicy and fluffy, this recipe provides a roasted twist on a classic. I love using new potatoes in this recipe, for an earthier flavour and crisp edge to the potatoes. Serve as a side dish to apple and ginger dhal (page 64).

Preheat the oven to 200°C/400°F/gas mark 6.

Mix together the chopped tomatoes, curry paste, turmeric, cumin and half the sliced chilli in the bottom of a large, deep roasting pan.

Place the halved new potatoes in the pan, then loosely cover with foil. Bake in the oven for 30 minutes, then remove the foil. Add the cherry tomatoes, then roast for a further 30 minutes until the potatoes are golden.

Remove from the oven and scatter with the remaining chilli and the coriander. Season with salt and pepper. Serve hot or cold.

EASY TIP:

These cooked potatoes will last for up to 3 days when kept in the fridge in a sealed container.

Gratin dauphinoise

SERVES 4 AS A SIDE

3 baking potatoes, peeled and very thinly sliced

200ml (generous ¾ cup) soya single (light) cream

200ml (generous ¾ cup) unsweetened soya milk

½ tsp fresh thyme leaves, finely chopped

1 garlic clove, crushed

pinch of grated nutmeg

generous pinch of sea salt and black pepper

Classic and surprisingly simple, these sliced potatoes are cooked in a creamy sauce, with lingering flavours of thyme, garlic and nutmeg. The perfect side dish for squash au vin (page 54) or as a sophisticated alternative to mashed potatoes with vegan sausages.

Preheat the oven to 200°C/400°F/gas mark 6.

Blot the potato slices with kitchen paper or a clean tea (dish) towel to remove the excess moisture. Arrange the slices over 3 layers in a deep roasting dish.

In a jug (pitcher), whisk together the soya cream, soya milk, thyme, garlic and nutmeg.

Pour the creamy sauce generously over the layered potatoes and cover loosely with foil. Bake in the oven for 1¼ hours.

Carefully remove and discard the foil, then return to the oven for a further 15 minutes.

Remove from the oven and season generously with salt and pepper before serving.

EASY TIP:

Use fresh thyme in this recipe for the best flavour and fragrance. Simply drag your thumb and finger down the length of the thyme sprig to easily remove the leaves.

Loaded nachos

with chive mayonnaise

SERVES 4

4 white tortilla wraps, sliced into triangles

2 tbsp sunflower oil

pinch of smoked paprika

100g (3½oz) medium-strength vegan cheese, grated

200g (7oz) canned black beans, drained and rinsed

4 cherry tomatoes, sliced

1 green chilli, finely sliced into rounds

2 small pickled gherkins, sliced into rounds

handful of fresh chives, finely chopped

2 rounded tbsp chilled vegan mayonnaise

pinch of sea salt

1 avocado, peeled, stoned and finely chopped

Serve these crisp, cheesy and spicy nachos with cooling chive mayonnaise, for the perfect dipping combination. Perfect as a starter to a Mexican-themed dinner, or as a moreish snack with drinks.

EASY TIP:

If you don't have black beans available, canned red kidney beans or green lentils make good alternatives.

Preheat the oven to 180°C/350°F/gas mark 4.

Arrange the tortilla triangles in a roasting pan and drizzle over the sunflower oil. Rub the oil over the triangles evenly. Sprinkle with smoked paprika, then bake in the oven for 5 minutes until just crisp.

Carefully remove the pan from the oven and sprinkle over the grated cheese, black beans, tomatoes, chilli and gherkins. Return to the oven and cook for a further 3–4 minutes until the cheese begins to melt.

Meanwhile, mix together the chives and mayonnaise in a small bowl. Season to taste with salt.

Remove the tortilla chips from the oven and transfer to a large serving plate. Scatter with avocado and spoon over the chive mayonnaise.

Rustic
hash browns

SERVES 4

2 tbsp sunflower oil

2 baking potatoes, scrubbed clean

2 spring onions (scallions), finely chopped

generous pinch of sea salt and black pepper

Hash browns are commonly associated with morning fry-ups. Crisp and golden on the outside and soft on the inside, they make the perfect addition to any vegan breakfast or brunch. These hash browns have an equally crisp outer and comforting flavour, without having to find the frying pan.

Preheat the oven to 180°C/350°F/gas mark 4. Drizzle the oil into a roasting pan and place in the oven while you prepare the potatoes.

Grate the potato onto a clean, dry tea (dish) towel or kitchen paper, then squeeze out as much moisture as possible. When no more moisture can be squeezed, tip the grated potato into a bowl.

Stir the spring onions through the grated potato and season generously with salt and pepper.

Shape hash brown rounds in your hands using 2 tablespoons of the mix, or press into a chef's ring for a neater, round finish.

Remove the hot roasting pan from the oven and use a flat slotted slice to place them in the hot oil. Bake in the oven for 20 minutes, then remove from the oven to carefully turn the hash browns. Return to the oven for a further 15–20 minutes until golden and crispy on the outside.

EASY TIP:

There's no need to peel the potatoes, simply scrub thoroughly, dry the potato and grate.

Sweet

Autumnal baked apples

SERVES 4

2 heaped tbsp sultanas
(golden raisins)

1 heaped tbsp dried
cranberries

1 tbsp roughly chopped
pecans

pinch of ground
cinnamon

pinch of grated nutmeg

2 tbsp maple syrup

4 large red eating
apples, core removed

Fill your kitchen with the aroma of baked
apples, cinnamon and maple syrup – perfect
for when those autumn nights start drawing in.
Serve with vegan vanilla ice cream and some
seasonal blackberries.

Preheat the oven to 180°C/350°F/gas mark 4.

In a bowl, stir together the sultanas, cranberries,
pecans, cinnamon, nutmeg and maple syrup.

Stand the cored apples upright in a small
roasting dish. Stuff the apples generously with
the sultana mix, then cover the dish loosely with
foil and bake in the oven for 25 minutes.

Carefully remove the foil and bake for a further
5 minutes until the filling is bubbling and the
apples are soft.

EASY TIP:

Kids will love to get involved with making this
easy dessert, especially mixing the cranberry
and pecan filling and stuffing the apples that
have been cored (by an adult or with close adult
supervision!).

Baked oat nests
with coconut yogurt and mango

MAKES 6

½ tsp sunflower oil, for greasing

1 ripe banana, peeled

2 tbsp maple syrup

pinch of ground cinnamon, plus extra to finish

100g (1 cup) rolled oats

6 tbsp thick coconut yogurt

½ ripe mango, peeled and sliced into thin 2cm (¾in) pieces

2 mint leaves, very finely sliced

Use a muffin tray (pan) to make these healthy breakfast nests, with tropical flavours of banana, mango and coconut yogurt. Perfect for mornings, or as a sweet snack at any time of the day.

Preheat the oven to 180°C/350°F/gas mark 4, then use a pastry brush to grease 6 holes of a muffin tray (pan).

In a bowl, mash the banana with a fork until semi-smooth. Add the maple syrup, cinnamon and oats, then stir until combined.

Take tablespoon-sized amounts of the mixture and press into the holes, following the shape of each individual cavity, so you form a hollow shell. Bake in the oven for 20–25 minutes until golden and crisp at the edges.

Remove from the oven and allow to cool before using a teaspoon to lift the oat cups out of the muffin holes.

Fill each oat cup with coconut yogurt, before placing slices of mango on top. Sprinkle with mint and dust over a pinch of cinnamon.

EASY TIP:

Save time in the morning by preparing the baked oat nests the day before. Store in a sealed container, then simply fill with yogurt and mango before serving.

Grilled peanut butter & strawberry sandwiches

SERVES 2

4 thick slices of white bread

1 tsp vegan butter

1 heaped tbsp crunchy peanut butter

2 tsp strawberry jam

4 strawberries, sliced into rounds, green tops discarded

There's no need to dig out the griddle pan or toasted sandwich maker, simply pop these tasty sandwiches on a baking sheet and cook in the oven, with minimal fuss.

Preheat the oven to 200°C/400°F/gas mark 6.

Lay out the bread on a clean surface and lightly butter one side of each slice.

Smooth peanut butter on the reverse sides of 2 slices, and spread jam on the unbuttered sides of the remaining two.

Lay the strawberry slices over the peanut butter and place the jam side facing into the strawberries. The buttered sides will be visible on the outside of each sandwich.

Place the sandwiches on a baking sheet and bake for 5–6 minutes, then flip the sandwiches over to bake for a further 5–6 minutes until golden and hot.

EASY TIP:

The sandwiches can be prepared the evening before and cooked the following morning, for a speedy and satisfying breakfast.

Low & slow rice pudding

SERVES 4

4 tbsp granulated sugar

1 tbsp good-quality vanilla paste

800ml (3⅓ cups) sweetened almond milk

pinch of grated nutmeg

100g (½ cup) pudding rice

2 tbsp flaked (slivered) almonds

If you love old-fashioned desserts, this baked rice pudding will hit the spot, with a creamy and rich sauce and a gentle wobble. Serve with jam or a sprinkle of demerara sugar or (my favourite way) with a spoonful of marmalade.

Preheat the oven to 150°C/300°F/gas mark 2.

In a bowl or jug (pitcher), lightly whisk together the sugar, vanilla paste, almond milk and nutmeg.

Tip the rice into a deep roasting pan or casserole dish, then pour over the milk mixture.

Bake in the oven for 2 hours, then sprinkle with flaked almonds before serving.

Pictured overleaf

EASY TIP:

Leave the rice pudding to cook for 2 hours for a fully baked version, or enjoy after 1¾ hours for a less set (yet still comforting) version.

Low & slow
rice pudding

Warm toffee butter

10 pitted dates

pinch of grated nutmeg

2 tbsp vegan butter

½ tsp good-quality vanilla extract

SERVES 4

Dates give this butter a caramelized, toffee flavour, making it the perfect condiment – spoon into porridge, on sweet waffles, vegan croissants, or simply spread on toast. Switch the nutmeg for cinnamon for a change.

Preheat the oven to 160°C/320°F/gas mark 3.

Place the dates in a roasting pan and sprinkle over a little grated nutmeg. Bake in the oven for 10–12 minutes until the dates are hot and softened.

Remove the dates from the oven and spoon into a high-powered blender or food processor. Add the vegan butter and vanilla extract and blitz until smooth and whipped.

Transfer to a clean jar and store in the fridge.

EASY TIP:

I love eating this butter while it's still warm, but it is also delicious enjoyed cold. Store in a sealed container in the fridge for up to 5 days.

Aperitif granita

SERVES 4

200ml (generous ¾ cup) good-quality smooth orange juice

100ml (scant ½ cup) Aperol

100ml (scant ½ cup) prosecco (ensure vegan)

juice of ½ unwaxed lemon

Put your roasting pan to good use – in the freezer! This Italian-inspired dessert is the perfect alternative to a classic Aperol Spritz, especially on a hot summer's day.

In a jug (pitcher), whisk together the orange juice, Aperol, prosecco and lemon juice. Pour the mix into a deep roasting pan (I also sometimes use a loaf tin), then freeze for 1 hour.

After 1 hour, use a fork to break up the ice, then return to the freezer for another hour.

After the second hour run a fork through the ice to separate and break the crystals. Return to the freezer again for another 30 minutes.

After the final 30 minutes, fork through the granita for a final time until all of the mixture is in icy crystals. Serve immediately.

Pictured overleaf

EASY TIP:

For a grown-up, boozy 'slush' drink, stir together equal measures of Aperol and prosecco with a dash of soda water, in a tall glass, then spoon in the granita.

Aperitif
granita

Cherry & almond crumble

SERVES 4

400g (14oz) pitted cherries (fresh or frozen; defrosted if frozen)

juice of ½ unwaxed lemon

2 tbsp maple syrup

100g (scant 1 cup) plain (all-purpose) flour

50g (½ cup) rolled oats

50g (¼ cup) demerara sugar

2 tbsp vegan butter

1 tbsp flaked (slivered) almonds

Juicy, hot cherries baked topped with an almond and oat crumble – desserts don't get much better than this. I've even been known to grate some dark chocolate into the cherries, for extra indulgence. Serve with vegan vanilla ice cream.

Preheat the oven to 200°C/400°F/gas mark 6.

Add the cherries to a deep roasting pan and spoon over the lemon juice and maple syrup.

In a bowl, stir together the flour, oats and sugar, then rub in the vegan butter with your fingertips until the mixture resembles breadcrumbs. Spoon the mixture onto a baking sheet in an even layer and scatter over the almonds.

Bake both the cherries and crumble in the oven for 12–15 minutes until the fruit is bubbling and the topping is golden.

Remove the from the oven and spoon the topping over the fruit just before serving.

EASY TIP:

I like to cook the topping on a separate baking sheet to the fruit, then sprinkle over just before serving, to keep the topping as crumbly and crisp as possible, but you can top the fruit with the crumble mix before baking, if you like, then bake them together in one dish.

Rustic blackberry & peach tart

SERVES 4

150g (5oz) blackberries

4 large peaches, stoned and sliced

1 tsp good-quality vanilla extract

1 tsp caster (superfine) sugar

1 sheet of shop-bought ready-rolled puff pastry (ensure dairy-free)

handful of small mint leaves

icing (confectioners') sugar, to dust

Enjoy this dessert in the late summer or early autumn, as a delicious taste of the changing seasons. Assemble the tart just before serving, as a fail-safe way to avoid a soggy base on the pastry. Serve with a drizzle of soya single cream, if you like.

Preheat the oven to 200°C/400°F/gas mark 6.

Add the blackberries, sliced peaches, vanilla extract and caster sugar to a deep roasting pan. Sprinkle over 2 teaspoons of water.

Unroll the puff pastry onto a baking sheet and roughly turn in the edges by 1cm to make a border. Prick the centre of the pastry with a fork.

Bake both the fruit and the pastry in the oven for 12–15 minutes until the fruit is bubbling and the pastry is golden. If the pastry centre rises up, gently push it down with a fork after baking.

Remove from the oven and evenly spoon the hot fruit over the pastry centre. Scatter with mint leaves just before serving then dust the tart with a little icing sugar.

EASY TIP:

Many brands of shop-bought puff pastry are accidentally vegan, as they use vegetable oil instead of butter, but always check the ingredients before you buy.

Whole roasted pineapple

with whipped coconut & rum

SERVES 4

Sweet, sticky, fruity and boozy – does a dessert get much better than this? This is great served at a summer get-together, but is fabulous on any day of the week. Use a thick, natural coconut yogurt, or chill a can of coconut milk and scoop off the rich cream.

Preheat the oven to 180°C/350°F/gas mark 4.

In a bowl, stir together the vegan butter, brown sugar and chilli flakes.

Place the whole pineapple in a deep roasting pan and dot the butter mix all over the flesh. Roast in the oven for 30 minutes, removing from the oven after 15 minutes to turn the pineapple and baste in the melted butter.

Meanwhile, whisk together the coconut yogurt and rum until combined.

Remove the roasted pineapple from the oven and squeeze over the lime juice. Serve with the whisked coconut and rum yogurt.

2 tbsp vegan butter

1 tsp soft light brown sugar

pinch of dried chilli flakes

1 ripe pineapple, skin peeled, green leafy top remaining (see Easy Tip)

4 tbsp thick coconut yogurt, chilled, or coconut cream

2 tsp rum

finely grated zest and juice of ½ unwaxed lime

EASY TIP:

To cut the skin off the pineapple, cut a flat base on the fruit then use a sharp knife to cut away the skin, from top to bottom, following the contours of the pineapple. The green top looks great in place when the dessert is served!

Lemon & poppy seed squares

MAKES 9 SQUARES

- SUITABLE FOR FREEZING, WITHOUT THE ICING

250g (2 cups) self-raising (rising) flour

100g (½ cup) caster (superfine) sugar

¾ tsp baking powder

1 tsp poppy seeds, plus extra to finish

250ml (1 cup) sweetened soya milk

100ml (scant ½ cup) sunflower oil

1 tsp good-quality vanilla extract

zest and juice of ½ unwaxed lemon

For the drizzle

zest and juice of ½ unwaxed lemon

150g (¾ cup) icing (confectioners') sugar

With a light and zesty sponge, topped with a sweet icing drizzle, these lemon squares are perfect for picnics and lunchboxes. The key to a light vegan sponge cake is not to over-stir the mixture, so use a light hand to fold in the liquid.

Preheat the oven to 180°C/350°F/gas mark 4. Line a shallow square roasting pan with baking parchment.

In a large bowl, stir together the flour, sugar, baking powder and poppy seeds. In a jug (pitcher), whisk together the soya milk, sunflower oil, vanilla extract, lemon zest and juice. Lightly fold the liquid mixture into the dry ingredients until just combined.

Pour into the lined roasting pan, then bake in the oven for 20–25 minutes until lightly golden and risen.

Meanwhile, prepare the drizzle. In a small bowl, mix together the lemon zest, juice and icing sugar until smooth. Set aside.

Remove the cake from the oven and allow to cool for a few minutes before turning out onto a wire rack. Once cool, drizzle over the icing, sprinkle on a few more poppy seeds, then slice into even squares.

EASY TIP:

These cake squares will keep for up to 3 days when stored in a sealed container, in a cool, dry place.

Apple pie flapjack

MAKES 9 SQUARES

4 tbsp sunflower oil

4 rounded tbsp golden syrup

½ tsp ground cinnamon

½ tsp grated nutmeg

150g (1½ cups) rolled oats

1 apple, grated, squeezed of excess juice

1 tbsp sultanas (golden raisins)

1 tbsp roughly chopped pecans

Two British pudding classics combined. All the flavours of apple pie, with the comfort of flapjack. This version eliminates the need to use a pan to melt vegan butter, as it's substituted for sunflower oil, which means reduced time – and less washing up! Just like any flapjack, it will become firmer as it cools, so allow it to drop to room temperature before slicing and enjoying.

Preheat the oven to 200°C/400°F/gas mark 6. Line a small roasting pan with baking parchment.

In a large bowl, mix together the oil, syrup, cinnamon and nutmeg until combined.

Stir in the oats, grated apple, sultanas and pecans until they are coated in the syrup mix.

Press the mixture into the lined roasting pan and smooth the top with the back of a spoon. Bake in the oven for 12 minutes, until the top is just golden. Allow to cool in the pan before slicing into squares.

EASY TIP:

This flapjack is delicious eaten as a snack, or crumble over vegan vanilla ice cream for a decadent dessert.

Index

Acknowledgements

Vegan Roasting Pan has been my favourite lockdown project, from testing the recipes in my kitchen (during the warmest summer months!), to being part of the shoot, albeit remotely via Zoom. As always, creating a beautiful book requires a team of hard-working and dedicated people – and I couldn't wish to be part of a better team.

I'd like to start with a big thank you to the editorial team at Quadrille. Thank you to publishing director Sarah Lavelle, for believing in this idea, and for all of the incredible opportunities over the past five years. Huge thank you to editor Harriet Webster for the smooth running of the project, attention to detail and sense of humour throughout. I can't wait to see you both again soon! Thank you to copy editor Clare Sayer for the editorial support. It is a privilege to work with you all.

Thank you to designer Emily Lapworth and team for the art direction and design. As always, your vision is fresh, modern and vibrant, and the outcome of the book is beautiful.

Massive thanks to photographer Luke Albert, food stylist Tamara Vos and assistants, and prop stylist Louie Waller for the socially-distanced shoot at Studio Boardroom. It was great to join you over Zoom and I can't wait to see you all again in person next time! The photographs are fantastic, thank you.

Heartfelt thank you to publicity manager Rebecca Smedley for your ongoing hard work with all the book campaigns – I can't wait until we can hit the road again! Thank you to marketing executive Laura Eldridge for your expertise, and for championing the books.

Huge thanks, as always, to my wonderful literary agent, Victoria Hobbs and the team at A.M. Heath. Without you, none of this would be possible and I am so grateful for your honesty, experience and guidance.

Thank you to my wonderful friends Mary-Anne, Emma, Charlotte, Louise, Amelia, Amy, Katie, Neil and Robert. You've all been amazing during lockdown, especially for checking up to make sure I'm taking a break when I forget to. I owe you all a coffee/wine very soon!

To my lovely and ever-supportive family: Mum, Dad, Carolyne and Mark. Thank you for your encouragement and kindness, I hope you enjoy the book. Thank you to my beautiful twin nieces Tamzin and Tara who fill me with inspiration and happiness. I look forward to seeing your creations now you're such confident and capable young cooks. Thank you to Auntie May for your kind words and support throughout the process.

In memory of Dudley, the adopted house rabbit, who has been the best writing partner and companion over the past 7 years. You are very missed, and will always be loved.

Publishing Director
Sarah Lavelle

Junior Commissioning Editor
Harriet Webster

Copy Editor
Clare Sayer

Art Direction & Design
Emily Lapworth

Photographer
Luke Albert

Food Stylist
Tamara Vos

Prop Stylist
Louie Waller

Make-up Artist
Dani Hooker

Head of Production
Stephen Lang

Production Controller
Sabina Atchia

First published in 2020 by Quadrille,
an imprint of Hardie Grant Publishing

Quadrille
52–54 Southwark Street
London SE1 1UN
quadrille.com

Text © Katy Beskow 2021
Photography © Luke Albert 2021
Design and layout © Quadrille 2021

The rights of Katy Beskow to be
identified as the author of this
work have been asserted by her
in accordance with the Copyright,
Design and Patents Act 1988.

Cataloguing in Publication Data:
a catalogue record for this book
is available from the British Library.

ISBN: 978 1 78713 702 8

Printed in China

MIX
Paper from
responsible sources
FSC™ C020056